EXECUTIVE ENGLISH/BOOK 2

By the same author: HOW TO SAY IT

Book 2

Executive English
Philip Binham

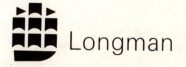

LONGMAN GROUP LIMITED
London

*Associated companies, branches and representatives
throughout the world*

© Longman Group Ltd (formerly
Longmans, Green & Co Ltd) 1969

All rights reserved. No part of this publication may be
reproduced, stored in a retrieval system, or transmitted
in any form or by any means, electronic, mechanical,
photocopying, recording, or otherwise, without
the prior permission of the Copyright owner.

First published 1969
New impressions *March, *October 1970;
*June 1971

ISBN 0 582 52421 0

Printed in Hong Kong by
Dai Nippon Printing Co (International) Ltd

Contents

Introduction vii

PART I
Management Techniques

1 Promotion and Command 2
2 The Effective Executive 7
3 The Boss and His Secretary 11
4 Looking for a Secretary 16
5 Personnel Problems 20
6 Talking about Labour 25
7 PR and Management 29
8 Call in the Consultant 35
9 The Manager and Change 39
10 Executive Meeting 44
11 Conference English 48
12 At a Conference 53

PART II
Manufacturer to Consumer

13 Export Services 60
14 Land, Sea and Air 66
15 Packaging—an Under-rated Technique 70
16 Talking about Packaging Materials 75
17 Hong Kong: Distribution Center 78
18 Manufacturer, Wholesaler, Retailer 84
19 The European Market Place (1) 87
20 Consumer Guidance 92
21 The European Market Place (2) 97
22 Consumer Motivation 101

GLOSSARY 106

Acknowledgements

We are grateful to the following for permission to reproduce copyright material:
The American Management Association Inc. for an adapted extract from 'Joint Venture: The Boss and His Secretary as a Business Team' by Eric Webster from *Management Review* February 1965, Copyright © 1965 by American Management Ass. Inc; British Institute of Management for adapted extracts from *The Manager* (the former journal of the British Inst. of Management) issues dated May and August 1964; Consumers' Association for an adapted extract from *Which?*; The Proprietors of *Distribution Manager* for an adapted extract from 'Hong Kong: Distribution Center' from issue dated October 1967; William Heinemann Ltd and Harper & Row Inc. for adapted extracts from *The Effective Executive* by Peter Drucker; author's agents, and William Heinemann Ltd for an adapted extract from *The Reality of Management* by Rosemary Stewart; author, and The Institute of Public Relations for an adapted extract from 'Public Relations and Management' by C. R. Bates from *Public Relations* April 1968; *International Trade Forum* for adapted extracts from 'London Venue for World's Exporters' by E. Ford from *Forum* September 1967, and 'Packaging – an Under-rated Technique' by P. Boissy from *Forum* November 1965 (published by International Trade Centre UNCTAD/GATT Geneva); Unilever Ltd for adapted extracts from 'The European Market Place' by Dr. E. Zahn from *Progress*, the Unilever Quarterly, September 1962.

We have been unable to contact the American copyright holders of *The Effective Executive* by Peter Drucker, and would appreciate any information that would enable us to do so.

We are also grateful to the following for permission to reproduce the illustrations:
Inbucon, pp. 3, 21, 37 and 41; Hughes Aircraft Co., California, p. 9; Evening News, p. 17; Barnaby's, pp. 31 and 79; Express Hotels, p. 49; *Marketing*, Haymarket Publishing Group, p. 55; Trans World Airlines, p. 61; The British Aluminium Co. Ltd., p. 67; John Walker and Sons Ltd., p. 71; Hoover Ltd., p. 89; *Which*, p. 93; J. Sainsbury Ltd., p. 103.

Introduction

General

This is the second of three books with tapes intended to teach the foreign student to understand and use the English language of business. Each book covers one year's work, providing material for two or three classroom hours per week, or one or two classroom hours plus one language laboratory hour. At the end of the third book the student should be able to understand *The Economist* and attend a business conference in English successfully.

Book 2 assumes that the student has already done four to five years of general English and has read *Executive English* Book 1 or some equivalent introductory book on business English. For classes that have not done Book 1, the teacher can check whether students have sufficient vocabulary for Book 2 by looking at the first question in the practice section of Chapters 1, 3, 5, etc. These are revision exercises largely based on the vocabulary of Book 1.

Except for the dialogues and Chapter 11 on Conference English, the book contains only genuine texts culled from articles and books. The texts have been doctored only where absolutely necessary; careful selection and copious notes keep the text within the students' range of comprehension.

Units

The basic unit of the book is a passage followed by NOTES and PRACTICE. Passages are followed up by dialogues on the same subject, so that the more colloquial spoken language of business is introduced side by side with the written language. Passages are carefully graded for length and difficulty.

Notes and vocabulary

After each chapter there are notes on the words and expressions that are likely to cause the student most difficulty. At the end of the book there is a vocabulary of business terms used.

Practice

After each chapter there is also a practice section including exercises on grammar and vocabulary, written and oral questions on the text and questions for discussion.

Tapes

There are 3 × 5" tapes, giving a total listening time of about 2 hours. The tapes, which are designed for use in a language laboratory, but which can also be used with a single tape-recorder in the classroom or at home, are divided into eleven lessons and cover all the Dialogues in the book, together with various forms of Practice based on the Dialogues.

Practice is provided in:
1 Intensive listening.
2 Taking part in conversation.
3 Use of various structural forms.

Notes for teachers

In the Practice exercises of several chapters, students are asked to make written or oral reports. These are intended to check on students' understanding of the passages, to cultivate intensive listening, and to develop a useful skill. The word *report* has been preferred to summary or précis, as indicating a practical activity where speed and fluency are more important than academic correctness. The technique for report making is explained step by step in Book 1. For classes that have not done this work before, techniques for note-taking and summarizing should be thoroughly explained in advance.

The abbreviations 'Am' and 'Br' are used in the NOTES to indicate American or British usage.

Part 1
Management Techniques

1 Promotion and Command

Letter to a Young Executive (1)

My dear Timothy,

I was glad to hear that you are to be given a more responsible job. The first step up is usually the hardest, but there are many good things about it. At your age a 'leg-up' is simple to understand. Your employers can only have one of two motives – either they want something done and think you are the right chap to do it, or they have sufficient interest in you to want to try you out. One thing they cannot be doing at this stage is getting you out of someone's way. Later on you will find promotion becomes more complex.

None of these things need worry you. If you turn out well you will confirm the judgment of the selectors, if not – it will hardly bring the company to the brink of disaster. But this does not mean you can wear your new responsibilities lightly. You must lose no time in adjusting yourself to your new powers and duties and to a changed relationship with your present colleagues.

Your first task must be to get a clear definition of what is expected of you and the extent of your powers, so that you can think clearly about what you are trying to achieve. I shall be most interested to hear of your progress and offer you my best wishes.

Your affectionate Godfather,
J. B. C. Miller-Bakewell

Letter to a Young Executive (2)

My dear Timothy,

Now that you are installed you have the opportunity to learn how to command. This means assessing a task and the resources needed to tackle it effectively, and making sure that whoever is set to do it understands the object, the method, and the means at his or her disposal. To be able to command effectively you must know the work of your department inside out and be able to do most of it at least as well as the majority of your staff – although there are special skills it would be pointless for you to acquire. What you need is a grasp of the principles involved, and an idea of the level of output of a competent performer.

Training a young executive

Once you really know what you are talking about and whether a job should take three hours or six to complete, you will have the basic confidence for effective command. Your staff will respect your knowledge and recognize that you are unlikely either to commit them to performing miracles or to fall for any scheme of featherbedding they may think up.

If you can use the opportunity to discuss your problems with your colleagues both to learn from them and to 'sell' the work of your own department by your quiet confidence in its quality, you will reap the full reward of effective command. You may also learn what other people can do to help you in time of need, but you must avoid giving the impression either that you are unable or unwilling to do it yourself. This may mean a lot of hard work in the early stages and you must bear in mind the story of the girl at the cocktail party who asked, 'How can I know what is "enough" until I have had too much?'

Your affectionate Godfather,
J. B. C. Miller-Bakewell
[<i>The Manager</i>, May 1964, p. 61 and
June 1964, p. 59]

NOTES

- 4 **step up**: move to a higher position in a firm, promotion.
- 5 **'leg-up'**: (colloquial) assistance in moving to a higher position.
- 7 **chap**: (colloquial) man.
- 8 **try you out**: see what you are capable of doing.
- 11 **turn out well**: succeed.
- 12 **judgment**: good sense, opinion, decision.
- 13 **brink**: edge.
- 13 **disaster**: great or sudden misfortune.
- 14 **wear ... lightly**: consider unimportant.
- 20 **godfather**: a man who promises at the baptism of someone else's child to help with the child's education, etc.
- 25 **installed**: placed in (your new) position.
- 27 **tackle**: deal with.
- 27 **set to do**: given the task of doing.
- 28 **at his ... disposal**: available.
- 30 **inside out**: completely, thoroughly.
- 32 **pointless**: quite unnecessary.

33 **grasp**: understanding.
34 **competent performer**: one who has enough ability, skill or knowledge to do a job properly.
38 **recognize**: realize, acknowledge, be prepared to admit.
38 **commit them to performing**: put them in a position where they are expected to perform.
39 **fall for**: deceived by.
39 **feather-bedding**: avoiding work, often by keeping more workers than the task really requires.
40 **think up**: invent.
42 **sell**: persuade others of the high quality of.
44 **reap the full reward of**: get the best results from.

Practice

1 Give your own definitions of what the following words and expressions mean as used in the letters above. Try to write your definitions first without looking the words up, then check your definitions against those given in the Vocabulary or Notes of *Executive English* Book 1 or in a dictionary.

responsible	extent	output
sufficient	achieve	scheme
stage	progress	bear in mind
promotion	resources	adjust
complex	involved	assess
deserve	acquire	staff

When you have checked your definitions, put the words and expressions in sentences of your own.

2 Choose the correct words from the following list and put them in the gaps in the sentences.

turn, task, inside, grasp, impression, confirm, commit, involved, brink, majority, extent, performing, definition.

a You must avoid giving the . . . that you are unwilling to help yourself.
b You must know the work of your department . . . out and be able to do most of it as well as the . . . of your staff.

5

c Your staff will recognize that you are unlikely to . . . them to . . . miracles.
d If you . . . out well, you will . . . the judgment of the selectors.
e Your first . . . must be to get a clear . . . of the . . . of your powers.
f What you need is a . . . of the principles. . . .
g You will hardly bring the company to the . . . of disaster.

3 Make notes on Letter 1, then write a summary of the letter of not more than one-third of the length of the original (about 120 words).

4 Answer these questions orally:

a Why has Timothy been given a 'leg-up'?
b Why do you think his relationship with his colleagues must change?
c What does learning to command in a firm include? Do you think it means other things besides those mentioned in the second letter?
d Why should a junior executive discuss problems with his colleagues?
e What did the girl at the cocktail party say? Do you agree with her?

5 Put yourself in Timothy's place and write a letter of about 200 words in reply to the second letter.

2 The Effective Executive

	Announcer:	This is B.B.C., Radio Four. Tonight, the first of our new series 'The Business World' begins, and Mary Owen, who writes for *The Executive Today*, is here to introduce the guest speaker.
5	*Owen:*	Good evening, and may I introduce Mr Peter F. Drucker, the well-known American management consultant and writer. Now, Mr Drucker, perhaps you would tell us what the main task of a business executive is.
10	*Drucker:*	Well, I'd say that his first job is to get the right things done – in other words he's expected to be effective.
	Owen:	D'you think it's possible to learn to be effective?
	Drucker:	Yes, I do. You see, effectiveness is a kind of habit. Call it a habit of mind if you like.
15	*Owen:*	Could you enlarge on that a bit please?
	Drucker:	Right. First, the executive needs to know where his time goes, and then make sure he's using what little time he can really call his own as usefully as possible.
20	*Owen:*	Yes, I can see that. Board meetings, wining and dining guests and so on must be great time consumers.
	Drucker:	They are. Then the executive has got to be interested in results. His first question must always be, 'What results are expected of me?'
25	*Owen:*	And what's the next ingredient in your recipe for the effective executive?
	Drucker:	He must build on strength, not weakness. He shouldn't worry about what his firm can't do. His job is to make sure it's doing what it can do as well as possible.
30	*Owen:*	Isn't it important too to concentrate on certain areas rather than spread his efforts too widely?
	Drucker:	That's certainly true. An executive's got to select a few major goals and give them priority all along the line.
	Owen:	You haven't said anything about decision making yet.
35	*Drucker:*	No, I've left that till last, though it's certainly not the least in importance. The big thing is, an executive shouldn't hurry his decisions.

Owen:	I suppose he has to be constantly making decisions?
Drucker:	He shouldn't need to. He should in fact need to make only few decisions, but they must be fundamental ones.
Owen:	So the main principle seems to be, do as little as possible as well as possible.
Drucker:	Very neat Miss Owen – I must remember that.
Owen:	Well, thank you very much Mr Drucker for your very clear exposition. I'm sure our listeners found it as interesting and instructive as I did.
Announcer:	The next programme in this series will be ....

[adapted from DRUCKER P. *The Effective Executive*. Heinemann, 1967. pp. 10–20]

NOTES

6 **management consultant**: person whose job is to give expert advice on management problems.
15 **enlarge on**: say something more about.
19 **board meetings**: meetings of the directors of a firm who belong to the Board of Directors and decide the policy of the firm.
19 **wining and dining**: entertaining.
20 **time consumers**: things that use up a lot of time.
24 **ingredient**: part of a whole. The ingredients of a cake are flour, butter, etc.
24 **recipe**: list of ingredients with instructions about their amounts, etc. Normally used in cooking.
32 **goals**: objects the firm tries to achieve; targets, objectives.
32 **give them priority**: arrange that they are the first things to be considered.
42 **neat**: said briefly and in an appropriate form.
44 **exposition**: presentation, explanation.
45 **instructive**: that instructs, teaches.

Practice

1 Re-tell the dialogue above in indirect speech. Try to vary the introductory verbs (say, ask, state, suggest, etc.). Remember that in English all verbs go into a past tense in indirect speech.

Do you think a bright young engineer should spend his most imaginative years on the same assignment?

Neither do we.

That's why we have a two-year Rotation Program for graduating engineers who would prefer to explore several technical areas. And that's why many of our areas are organized by function—rather than by project.

At Hughes, you might work on spacecraft, communications satellites and/or tactical missiles during your first two years.

All you need is an EE, ME or Physics degree and talent.

If you qualify, we'll arrange for you to work on several different assignments...and *you* can help pick them.

You may select specialized jobs, or broad systems-type jobs. Or you can choose not to change assignments if you'd rather develop in-depth skills in one area.

Either way, we think you'll like the Hughes approach.

It means you'll become more versatile in a shorter time. (And your salary will show it.)

```
------------------
| HUGHES         |
------------------
HUGHES AIRCRAFT COMPANY
AEROSPACE DIVISIONS
```

2 After studying the dialogue carefully or listening several times to the recording of the dialogue on the tapes that go with this book, one student reads the part of Mary Owen, while another with book closed takes the part of Peter Drucker. If necessary the class can be divided into pairs so that all can do the exercise simultaneously.

3 The class is divided into pairs, who together practise 'radio interviews' lasting three to five minutes. Each pair chooses a subject from the following. All subjects have been dealt with in Book 1. Students should have time to prepare this exercise.

a Marketing new products in your country.
b Overseas agents.
c Your country as an importer.
d Your country's exports.
e Prestige jobs in your country.
f Kinds of publicity available in your country.
g Language difficulties in exporting.

4 Try, without looking at the dialogue, to list the habits of mind mentioned by Mr Drucker. Add any others you may think of.

5 Give as many examples as you can find of 'time consumers' in the life of:

a yourself
b a managing director
c a housewife
d a teacher
e a manual worker
f a clerk

3 The Boss and His Secretary

Joint Venture

A recent article in the business press declared that a good secretary can make a $15,000-a-year man worth $20,000, and that a bad secretary can reduce his value to $10,000. Any executive should recognize this as an undeniable under-statement.

Backed by a good secretary, many a man without spectacular talents, but with the good sense not to thwart her, has achieved heights of eminence and power undreamed of by his less fortunate colleagues. On the other hand, anyone who has experienced the misery of ill-typed letters, appointments missed, and excuses given with more truth than tact – 'I know it's 3:15, Mr Carter, but he's still out to lunch' – will know that the personal secretary makes the difference between riches and ruin.

The Ideal Secretary

What would every man consciously or unconsciously like to find in his secretary?

Loyalty is the first requirement. If a man can't trust his secretary, whom can he trust? No relationship in business involves a higher degree of trust and responsibility between two persons than the secretary-boss-team.

Next, *conscience*. Secretaries are seldom paid what they deserve or what they are worth, though conditions are improving. Consequently, there is little except her conscience to insure that long hours are kept when necessary, things are done properly, and no loose ends are left untied.

Next we come to *initiative*. A secretary should be able to act for her boss in his absence in many of the fields in which he operates. Again, most executives at some time or other become overworked or non-objective and may miss obvious courses of action. A secretary should not permit her boss to make obvious mistakes. On the other hand, he should be consulted before a major action is taken. In fact, true initiative is the ability to know when to act on your own and when to consult.

Ability to write. Every secretary should at least be capable of handling routine correspondence for her boss and avoiding mistakes in English and in spelling. It is preferable, of course, if she has a real ability to write – to do reports and summaries and take good minutes of involved meetings. Well-educated women often have considerable talent in this direction, and whatever talent there is should be used to the full.

Tact and charm. Business can be tense, and tempers often get frayed. A girl who can not only avoid friction but actually reduce it is of great value.

Good dress sense and presentation. This involves looking and sounding attractive, yet never provoking unnecessary attention. A secretary is a man's status symbol. You may deplore this, but it is a fact of life, and on his status depend his income and his success.

Psychological insight is another requirement. It involves understanding what makes people tick, being able to make predictions about their behavior in given sets of circumstances, understanding the boss's moods – and, within limits, helping to soothe him out of them and to forgive him for them.

A good educational background is another plus value. It is immensely useful to have people who know things around you.

Of course, the executive who finds all these traits in his secretary is fortunate indeed.

The Power Behind the Throne

The importance of the secretary in the business world has been gravely underestimated, and only now it is beginning to be reappraised. When it becomes necessary to change systems or introduce reform, for example, it is always useful to call the executives concerned together and explain to them what is to be done. It is often even more useful to call their secretaries together afterwards and explain the whole thing to them. Invariably, when that is done, the change works.

[ERIC WEBSTER 'Joint Venture'.
Management Review, Feb 1965, pp. 36–42]

NOTES

title **joint:** done by two or more persons, combined.

title **venture:** undertaking involving uncertainty, business enterprise in which loss is risked in the hope of profit.

5 **under-statement:** statement that says less than the facts indicate. The opposite is *exaggeration*.

6 **backed:** supported. The noun is *backing:* Due to insufficient backing the project had to be abandoned.

7 **thwart:** obstruct, oppose, frustrate, prevent from acting.

8 **heights of eminence:** high position.

10 **ill-typed:** badly typed.

11 **3:15:** American punctuation. British: 3.15. Compare behavior (line 50), British: behaviour.

25 **loose ends are left untied:** work (business) that should be completed is left undone.

29 **non-objective:** objective = seeing things from outside, without becoming involved personally. Thus *non-objective* means taking things too personally.

31 **consulted:** asked for advice.

38 **minutes:** official record of what is said and done at a meeting.

38 **involved:** here: complicated.

41 **be tense:** involve nervous strain.

41 **tempers ... get frayed:** people become bad-tempered, lose their tempers.

42 **friction:** difficult situations, arguments, differences of opinion leading to quarrels.

44 **dress sense:** ability to dress well, to wear clothes attractively.

44 **presentation:** being suitable in appearance, manners, etc. Adjective: *presentable:* 'Now children, try and look presentable, your father will be home soon!'

45 **provoking:** giving cause for, arousing.

46 **deplore this:** think this is a bad thing.

48 **insight:** power to see into and understand.

49 **what makes people tick:** what is the driving force in people, what they are like, why they act as they do. (A clock is driven by a spring, which causes the 'ticking' sound.)

50 **given sets of circumstances:** circumstances of certain kinds.

51 **moods:** states of mind. Here = bad moods.

51 **soothe him out of them:** comfort him so that he is in a good mood.

53 **plus value:** value that increases one's worth.

57 **power behind the throne:** person who has power although he (she) is not the 'official' leader (boss, king).

59 **reappraised:** considered in a new light.

65 **works:** is successful.

13

Practice

1 Give your own definitions of the meaning of the following as they are used in the above passage. Write your own definitions first, then look the words up to check their meaning.

team	report	initiative
the press	summary	tact
undeniable	talent	loyalty
spectacular	charm	insure
ruin	status symbol	underestimate
consciously	prediction	reform
degree	trait	major

When you have checked your definitions, put the words and expressions in sentences of your own.

2a Make nouns from the following verbs and adjectives and use your nouns in sentences of your own.

declare	responsible	consult
reduce	absent	capable
recognize	operate	correspond
achieve	permit	prefer
attract	succeed	predict
behave	forgive	grave

b Make adjectives from the following nouns and verbs, and use your adjectives in sentences of your own.

misery	conscience	ability
truth	deplore	prefer
loyalty	explain	recognize
trust	permit	attraction

3 Make notes for a report on this passage, then write a report of not more than one-third the length of the original.

4 There are two sub-titles in this passage:

The Ideal Secretary
The Power Behind the Throne

Find new sub-titles instead of them.

5 Answer the following orally:

a What are the main requirements of a good secretary?
b What kinds of writing is it desirable for a secretary to be able to do?
c What does psychological insight involve for a secretary?
d Why do you think it is important to explain to secretaries what is to be done when changing systems and introducing reform?

6 Questions for discussion:

a Throughout this passage the boss has been referred to as 'he' and the secretary as 'she'. Are all bosses men and all secretaries women in your country? Do you think they should be? Why?
b Do you think many secretaries in your country have the qualities of the 'ideal secretary' in this passage? What would you say are their chief failings?
c If you were a secretary, what qualities would you expect of your boss? Do you think many bosses would come up to your expectations in your country? What would you say are their chief failings?
d What are secretaries paid in your country? Do you consider this adequate?

4 Looking for a Secretary

David Simpson, whom we met when he was interviewed for a job (Book 1, Chapter 5), is now Export Manager of a canned foods factory. He needs a capable secretary, and now has the task of acting as interviewer himself. The applicant he is interviewing at present is Victoria Honeyworth.

Simpson: Please sit down Miss Honeyworth. Smoke?
Honeyworth: No thank you, not just now.
Simpson: Well, I think you probably have a fair idea what sort of job you've applied for.
Honeyworth: Yes, it was very clearly explained in the advertisement for applications.
Simpson: I see from your application you've had quite a lot of experience as a secretary already.
Honeyworth: Yes, I've been a secretary for five years, in three different firms.
Simpson: You've changed firms quite often.
Honeyworth: Yes, I wanted to get more interesting work – that's why I'm applying for this post.
Simpson: Good. Now, perhaps you would tell me what sort of qualities you'd look for in your secretary if you were in my shoes.
Honeyworth: Well, to start off with, I'd say she needs to be pretty hard-working.
Simpson: Yes – as a matter of fact I'm new to this job myself, but so far I certainly haven't had too much time on my hands. Anything else?
Honeyworth: I've learnt that the secretary of an export manager has to be able to do a lot of things on her own initiative.
Simpson: Quite. By the way, d'you like travelling?
Honeyworth: Oh yes, especially abroad – and I speak French and German fairly fluently.
Simpson: Excellent. You'd probably have to come along with me to conferences and things on the Continent from time to time.

Bosses come nicer through the Evening News small-ads

Honeyworth: I'd like that very much.
Simpson: Now I see from the report the Personnel Department sent me that you did reasonably well in the shorthand and typing test, and very well indeed in the intelligence test. I suppose you'd be able to handle report writing – summaries, keeping minutes at meetings and so on?
Honeyworth: Yes, I've had to do quite a lot of that kind of work, and I seem to have a better memory than average.
Simpson: Yes, I can see that from your test results, and you'd certainly need it as my secretary because my memory's like a sieve. And what about planning the manager's day?
Honeyworth: I'm used to doing that, and to seeing that he doesn't forget his appointments.
Simpson: That sounds fine. By the way, how d'you feel about sharing an office room with your boss? We're a bit short of space here as you can see.
Honeyworth: From the secretary's point of view I think it's much better – there's not much chance of her superior forgetting to let her know about important matters.
Simpson: Yes, I rather agree. Well, thank you very much Miss Honeyworth, and you'll be hearing from us in the next few days.
Honeyworth: Thank you – and I certainly hope the answer will be favourable.

NOTES

2 **canned**: also tinned.
3 **capable**: able to do the job well.
8 **fair**: quite good.
18 **post**: job, position.
21 **in my shoes**: in my position.
25 **time on my hands**: leisure time, time to spare.
28 **on her own initiative**: by herself, without anyone telling her what to do.
34 **the Continent**: Europe, especially Western Europe.
37 **Personnel Department**: department concerned with matters to do with those employed by the firm.

38 **shorthand**: Am. stenography.
41 **keeping minutes**: writing a report on what is said and done at a meeting.
47 **like a sieve**: will not hold anything, i.e. a very poor memory.
55 **superior**: person above an employee.

Practice

1 Re-tell the above dialogue in indirect speech.

2 After studying the dialogue carefully, two students with books closed take the parts of David Simpson and Victoria Honeyworth.

3 The class is divided into pairs, who together practise interviews for jobs. Suggested jobs:

a a managing director
b a typist
c an agent
d an export manager
e an interpreter
f an office clerk
g a travelling salesman
h a shop-assistant

4 Discuss the advantages and disadvantages of a secretary sharing the boss's room.

5 Personnel Problems

Letter to a Young Executive (3)

My dear Timothy,

I was delighted to hear about the way your department is shaping, and particularly of the personal relationship you have begun to establish with your staff and your colleagues. The fact that you have a scheme for improvement in hand already is also a good sign, but I must warn you that to be too much of a new broom doesn't always mean that you get to the head of the queue any faster.

If you are going to be successful as an innovator there are two things to be borne in mind. First of all you must make sure that what you propose to do is right and then stick to it. Secondly, once convinced that it is right, do not be diffident about enlisting the assistance of your superiors.

Patience means waiting until the moment at which your effort will be most effective, and using the waiting time as fruitfully as possible. Even so, impatience is a most valuable characteristic in an executive. Patience with people is quite different from patience with problems because people are much more changeable. Patience with people means a gentle pressure towards improvement in performance, pressure which can be intensified when all the circumstances are favourable.

Of course it's up to you to make the circumstances favourable. This is what managers are for.

Your affectionate Godfather,
J. B. C. Miller-Bakewell

Letter to a Young Executive (4)

My dear Timothy,

Thank you very much for your letters. So sorry that you are losing your best clerk through 'natural increase' and just as she was becoming really useful. This has been happening earlier and earlier as the years go by. Your Uncle Arthur nearly had a fit when girls left to get married at thirty, perhaps because he was not exactly one for permanent attachments himself.

Aptitude test for a future employee

The expansion in higher education, the strong tendency to stay longer at school, higher earnings and earlier marriage are all reducing the supply and shortening the working life of able young women. Later return is only a partial solution to the problem. What with one thing and another it might be argued that the computer age has arrived only in the nick of time. You must recognize this and play your cards accordingly.

I am not sure whether you have much choice in the selection of your staff. If you are allowed any freedom of choice, be sure to ask yourself the key question: 'How quickly can I turn this girl into a skilled member of my department?' Whatever the quality of the material available, get a detailed plan of training ready and treat its execution as a matter of urgency. The loss of a senior member of staff should have given you the opportunity to re-allocate the duties of the team to make some jobs more satisfying and others easier to learn quickly. What matters is not so much the length of service, but how large a proportion of it can be a positive contribution to the work of the department. Next time someone leaves you will be able to say 'We were lucky to reap the rewards of training her for so long'. Uncle Arthur never quite reached that stage. . . .

Your affectionate Godfather,
J. B. C. Miller-Bakewell

[*The Manager*, August 1964, p. 51 and September 1964, p. 59]

NOTES

3 **shaping**: showing signs of development.

5 **establish**: make.

6 **in hand**: started.

7 **new broom**: *a new broom sweeps clean* is an English saying. Here: a person newly in authority who tries to make changes.

8 **the head of the queue**: the job at the top.

9 **innovator**: one who introduces new ideas.

11 **stick to**: keep to, continue to support.

11 **once**: when you are finally.

12 **diffident**: shy, hesitant.

12 **enlisting the assistance**: obtaining the help.

13 **your superiors**: those higher than you. Those below you are your *subordinates*.
15 **fruitfully**: usefully.
20 **intensified**: increased.
22 **it's up to you**: it is your responsibility, it is your business.
29 **'natural increase'**: she is going to have a baby.
31 **nearly had a fit**: was very upset.
37 **later return**: leaving work for some years (while the children are small) and coming back to it later.
37 **what with one thing and another**: since there are so many difficulties.
39 **in the nick of time**: just in time.
40 **play your cards**: behave, make your plans.
43 **key**: essential, important, central, vital.
43 **turn . . . into**: make.
46 **execution**: putting into practice.
46 **matter of urgency**: something to be done as quickly as possible.
46 **senior**: more important, higher.
47 **re-allocate**: share out, distribute in a new way.
49 **service**: period spent working for the firm.

Practice

1 Give your own definitions of the meaning of the following as they are used in the above letters. Write your own definitions first, then look the words up to check their meaning.

relationship	permanent	pressure
staff	tendency	choice
colleague	partial	clerk
scheme	solution	supply
warn	contribution	partial
be convinced	reap the rewards	patience

When you have checked your definitions, put the words and expressions in sentences of your own.

2 Fill in the prepositions in the following:

a Do not be diffident . . . enlisting the assistance . . . your superiors.
b It's up . . . you to make the circumstances favourable. This is what managers are . . . .

  c The computer age has arrived . . . the nick . . . time.
  d I was delighted to hear . . . the relationship you have established . . . your staff.
  e Bear . . . mind that you should stick . . . what you propose to do.
  f This means a gentle pressure . . . improvement . . . performance.
  g As the years go . . ., more and more clerks are being lost . . . 'natural increase'.
  h The expansion . . . education shortens the working life . . . able young women.

3 Students' books closed. The teacher reads aloud about five lines (two sentences) of either the first or the second letter, then pauses while the students make notes on what has been read. After the letter has been read, students (keeping their books closed) write reports from their notes of not more than one-third the length of the original.

4 Answer the following orally:

  a What things must be borne in mind if one wants to be successful as an innovator?
  b Why is the working life of women shorter nowadays than formerly?
  c What do you think are the disadvantages of 'later return' by women?
  d What has the coming of the computer age to do with the female employment question?
  e In what ways do you think a manager can make circumstances more favourable in order to get better staff performance?

5 Write an essay of 400–600 words on 'Female Employment in My Country'.

6 Talking about Labour

Announcer: This is B.B.C., Radio Four. In the second programme of 'The Business World' the guest speakers are Mr Martin Dean, Managing Director of a large paper mill, and Mr Henry Benfield, who works in a furniture factory. Mary Owen, who has herself been a Personnel Manager, will lead the discussion.

Owen: The first question I'd like to discuss is, what do you think are the most effective ways of getting the best out of the personnel of a company? Mr Dean.

Dean: That's a broad question of course, but in my experience I'd say incentives like profit-sharing schemes can be very useful. We've been running one of these schemes for several years, and we believe our productivity's improved a lot because of it.

Owen: What would you say about this, Mr Benfield?

Benfield: Well, speaking as a worker myself, as I see it these new schemes and fringe benefits and that are all very nice, but a good steady wage that keeps up with the cost-of-living and reasonable working hours are what most of the chaps I know want.

Owen: I'd like to put in a word for good information too. Running a house magazine for the employees can be useful to help give the workers a sense of belonging. Then I think it's a good idea to get some of the management to visit the workers on social occasions and speak to them.

Benfield: What about the workers visiting the bosses on social occasions to speak to them?

Dean: You know, that might be rather interesting.

Owen: Then I'd like to ask you gentlemen what you feel about woman labour?

Benfield: My answer to that is, let the women work as much as they want to – my wife's had a job ever since we got married – just as long as they don't take jobs away from men that need them.

Owen: What about equal pay?

	Benfield:	No, I don't agree with that. After all, it's the man who's got the responsibility of feeding the family, isn't it?
40	*Dean:*	But if women are paid less than men, isn't there a danger that management is more likely to employ women so they can save on the wage bill?
	Benfield:	Well, yes, I suppose you're right. Funny, I never thought of it that way.
	Owen:	What do you feel about employing women, Mr Dean?
45	*Dean:*	Well, on the whole women do a very good job of work, but they do have a shorter working life than men – many of them stop working when they get married, they have babies and so on. And one thing that's struck me is that young women in particular seem to pick up
50		every possible illness that's going – from their children at home I suppose.
	Owen:	Well, I suppose I ought to stick up for my own sex after all these masculine opinions. I'd certainly say from what I've seen and heard that women are often
55		more conscientious than men, and they're not so likely to go on strike and follow the Unions like a flock of sheep.
	Benfield:	Here, that's not fair you know. If a working man doesn't support his Union, he's letting the other lads
60		down, and he's putting himself in a position where he's got no protection from the bosses at all.
	Owen:	Yes, the Unions have their uses of course. Well, there were lots of other things I'd have liked to ask your opinion about – overtime, re-training, mobility of
65		labour and so on, but they'll have to wait because our time's up, so thank you very much, and goodnight everybody.
	Announcer:	You have been listening to . . .

NOTES

3 **mill**: factory.

11 **incentives**: ways of encouraging people to work harder.

11 **profit-sharing**: a system whereby all employees of a firm get a percentage of the profits, so that if the profits are high, the employees' earnings also rise.

17 **fringe benefits**: advantages given to workers by the firm in other forms than wages, e.g. free medical care.
18 **steady**: that can be relied upon, that does not drop or end suddenly.
19 **reasonable**: moderate, not too long.
22 **house magazine**: a publication for members of the firm only.
41 **wage bill**: the amount of money the firm must pay out in the form of wages and salaries.
42 **funny**: strange.
52 **stick up for**: support.
55 **conscientious**: careful, honest, painstaking.
56 **strike**: organized refusal to work in order to compel an employer to agree to workers' demands.
56 **the Unions**: the Trade Unions, the organizations who look after the rights of workers.
58 **fair**: just.
59/60 **letting ... down**: failing to support, betraying.
59 **lads**: (colloquial) men.
64 **overtime**: working longer hours than normally.
64 **re-training**: teaching workers new trades, or new skills for their present jobs.
64 **mobility**: willingness to move from one place or job to another.
65 **our time's up**: we have no more time.

Practice

1 A panel discussion (see Book 1 Chapter 10 and Book 2 Chapter 20). Students are chosen to be on a panel of three to four persons, and a Chairman is appointed. The general subject for discussion is 'The Boss versus the Worker', and the panel is required to answer such questions as:

a Do you believe in profit-sharing?
b What do you think about the most important fringe benefits?
c Should all industry be socialized?
d What do you feel about woman labour?
e What incentives can an employer offer his employees?
f Is the five-day week a good idea?
g Should workers be required legally to work overtime when necessary?
h Should all workers belong to a Trade Union?
i Should women get equal pay?

Students can be asked to supply further questions as required. The teacher can decide whether or not the panel are given an opportunity to prepare their answers.

2 Questions for general discussion:

a What arrangements for re-training of personnel are offered in your country in various fields either by private or public organizations?

b Is labour mobile in your country? Should it be? Or should factories, etc. be established where surplus labour is available?

7 PR and Management

It is an inescapable fact that the term 'public relations' has an unpleasant ring in the ears of most people. To use its own jargon, it could do with a better 'public image'. This could be because there is something in the British character which dislikes anything which seems to be like trumpet blowing; or at least we like to make out that this is the case.

However, there is a great deal of confusion about the difference between boasting and communicating. For example, consider the following – 'The United Kingdom exports twice as much per head of population as Japan' or 'in the last year or two we have become the fastest growing computer market in Europe' or 'our progress in management training courses at universities is now the envy of Europe'. Items like these don't sound too bad at all and certainly help to boost morale. Is it therefore a bad thing to publicise facts like these?

Why don't the newspapers publish such items? Is it the fault of the press that strikes, lay-offs, downward trends in productivity seem to be the only items worthy of print; or is it that management seldom does enough to keep contact with the press, to make its points, and to put things in their proper perspective?

It is particularly in connection with labour troubles that management is most wary about publicity, and is less articulate than at any other time. And it is equally the time when labour has the least inhibitions and is the most vociferous and gets the most publicity. If you want to win an election you have to get your message through to the mass of voters. But it seems that whenever management wants to break through restrictive practices, it holds its negotiations behind closed doors.

Why is it that managing directors are so inaccessible to industrial correspondents? News releases, if given at all seem to be entirely confined to news about an order having been recently received, or personnel changes. Surely there are many other areas of mutual interest between management, the press or the public.

Why This Reluctance?

Perhaps the reluctance of managers to handle the task of public relations is that it takes too much planning and thinking about. And yet planning and careful thinking is one of the main fundamentals of management.

It is widely recognized that publicity is a valuable aid to management. But it is not often recognized that publicity is also an extremely powerful tool of management. Giving the right information, or in other words projecting the right 'image', can so easily pave the way for improved labour relations, ease the problem of attracting the best recruits, and can attract favourable attention which can yield many other indirect benefits.

Public relations is not confined to getting mentions in the press, or to the adoption of specialized techniques of advertising. PR work embraces such things as the appearance of your entrance hall, your notepaper, internal communications about the work of various departments, and the general activities and successes of the company as a whole. This means that all who have contact with the company get a favourable impression – it is rather like the young lad who brushes his hair extra carefully when he goes out to see his girlfriend. He recognizes, and so should we all, that appearances are vitally important.

Dispelling an Illusion

Let me dispel any illusions that public relations work for the projection of a good company image is deceitful or cynical. Although it is possible, by using expert PR work, to create a particular image about a company, it won't be long before any distortion of the truth becomes widely known.

It is no use pretending that public relations work is a simple subject to master. However, it is one about which every managing director should have a fair understanding. It requires much more subtlety than merely holding cocktail parties and filling reporters with gin. Nevertheless, top management should make it their business to meet the press for the purpose of seeking out subjects of mutual interest, so as to utilise the tremendous power of the many channels of communication which are available.

[BATES, C. R. 'Public Relations and Management'. *Public Relations*, April 1968]

Information session for industrial correspondents

NOTES

title **public relations**: planned effort to establish and maintain mutual understanding between an organization and its public.
2 **jargon**: special language used in a trade, profession or other group. The word is often used contemptuously.
5 **trumpet blowing**: to blow one's own trumpet is to boast about oneself.
5 **make out**: explain, claim.
8 **communicating**: sharing one's ideas with someone else.
12 **envy**: desire for some advantage possessed by another.
14 **boost**: raise, make stronger.
14 **morale**: spirit. 'After the victory the army's morale was high.'
17 **lay-offs**: no longer employing workers because there is no work for them to do. The management of a factory sometimes has to lay off some of its employees.
20 **put in ... perspective**: see things in proportion.
22 **wary**: careful, cautious.
22 **is less articulate**: does not give clear information.
24 **inhibitions**: unwillingness to act or speak.
24 **vociferous**: noisy.
27 **restrictive practices**: a number of trade practices (controlled by law under the Restrictive Trade Practices Act of 1956) such as joint action by manufacturers against a retailer who had sold the product of one of them at a price lower than that fixed by the manufacturer concerned.
29 **inaccessible to**: hard to meet for.
30 **news releases**: prepared information given to the press
35 **reluctance**: unwillingness, hesitation.
42 **projecting the right 'image'**: giving the right picture.
42 **pave the way**: prepare the way.
56 **dispelling**: removing.
57 **illusion**: false impression or belief.
58 **deceitful**: intended to deceive, to give a false picture.
60 **distortion**: pulling out of shape, changing to give an untrue picture.
64 **fair**: quite good.
65 **subtlety**: cleverness.

Practice

1 Give your own definitions of the meanings of the following as they are used in the above passage. Write your own definitions first, then look the words up to check their meaning.

inescapable	the press	mutual
image	downward trend	fundamental
confusion	to master	recruit
boast	message	yield
the United Kingdom	negotiations	a mention
computer	correspondent	embrace
item	confined	vitally
publicize	personnel	cynical

2 Fill in the blanks with words or expressions that you feel are suitable:

a Why are directors so often ... to newspaper correspondents; is their ... due to shyness?
b A director should have a fair ... of public relations, although it is not a simple ... to ... .
c There is something in the British ... that dislikes ... blowing, or at least we like to ... out that this is the ... .
d It is particularly in ... with labour ... that management is most ... about publicity.
e PR work ... such things as the ... of your entrance hall, internal ... about the work of various ... and so on.
f Top ... should make it their ... to meet the press for the ... of seeking ... subjects of mutual ... .
g Let me ... any illusions that PR work for the ... of a good image is ... .
h Is it the ... of the press that strikes and lay-offs seem to be the only ... worthy of print?

3 The teacher reads once about five lines of the passage, then pauses while the students make notes. After the teacher has read about thirty lines, students have time to re-read their notes and then give oral reports of about one-third the length of the original. This exercise can be done in the language laboratory if desired.

4 Answer the following orally:

a Do you agree that the term 'public relations' has an unpleasant ring in the ears of most people? Give reasons for your answer.
b Do you think the quotations between lines 9–13 are boastful? Should such items be published in newspapers?

c What is the relation between the business world and the press in your country?
d Why are managers often reluctant to handle the tasks of PR?
e Mention as many things as you can think of that PR embraces.
f Do you consider that the PR of firms, etc. that you have come across is in any way deceitful?

5 There are two sub-titles in this passage:

Why This Reluctance?
Dispelling an Illusion

Find alternative sub-titles to replace them.

6 Write an essay of 400–600 words on 'PR in My Country'.

8 Call in the Consultant

David Simpson has been given the task of reorganizing the Export Department of his company. He and the Managing Director have agreed that it might be best to call in a Management Consultant to decide what must be done.

5 *Secretary:* Mr Rank, the consultant, is waiting to see you Mr Simpson.
Simpson: Thank you Miss Honeyworth. Please ask him to come in. – Ah, how d'you do Mr Rank. – This is my secretary, Miss Honeyworth.
Rank and
10 *Secretary:* How d'you do.
Simpson: I thought we might get Miss Honeyworth to make a few notes of things as they come up, if that's all right by you.
Rank: Of course. Excellent idea.
15 *Simpson:* Right. Now what I think we'd better do to start with is just clear the ground a bit, so perhaps I could ask you a few questions.
Rank: Well, I can't guarantee to answer them all, but fire away.
20 *Simpson:* Well, first of all, the usual question – what's your normal charge for this kind of job? D'you have a standard fee?
Rank: No – we'd have to make a thorough preliminary study before we could give a precise figure.
25 *Simpson:* Quite, but before we can get started my superiors'll want to see some sort of approximate budget. Could we work something out d'you think?
Rank: Our usual practice is to draw up a letter of agreement stating our estimated fee, together with expenses.
30 *Simpson:* Could you tell me a bit more about your expenses?
Rank: They normally come to between ten and fifteen per cent of the fee.
Simpson: Good. And could you also put in an estimate of how long the job's likely to take?

35	Rank:	Certainly. Then I'd like to propose that we draw up a plan of study.
	Simpson:	What kind of things would that cover?
	Rank:	It would state for example who'd do the work, and the type of report to be finally submitted.
40	Simpson:	Splendid. Have you got all that Miss Honeyworth?
	Secretary:	Yes Mr Simpson. By the way, there was one point you asked me to remind you about.
	Simpson:	She's my memory you know, Mr Rank.
	Rank:	And a very – er – capable memory I'm sure.
45	Simpson:	Yes, what was it?
	Secretary:	It was about how we can best get our employees in general to cooperate with the consultants.
	Rank:	That's a very good point, but I think it can only be answered when we've had a closer look at your department. The main thing is that you're aware that our recommendations may lead to some criticism and discontent among your staff. We may even have to recommend your sacking some people, though of course it'll be up to you whether you take our advice or not.
55	Simpson:	No, if we decide to use your services, we'll follow your recommendations all right. After all, you're the experts.
	Rank:	Well, I hope your colleagues'll agree with you when the time comes to make some decisions that may not be too pleasant. It's not always easy to convince managing directors that they may not know what's best for their company you know.
	Simpson:	No, I can believe that. Anyway, I think that's exhausted our questions for the moment, hasn't it Miss Honeyworth?
	Secretary:	That was all you mentioned Mr Simpson.
	Simpson:	Good. Then perhaps you'd get the files in please, and we'll get started right away. Oh yes, one thing – you'll have lunch with me today, won't you Mr Rank?
70	Rank:	With pleasure.
	Simpson:	Just ring through to the canteen and make sure they've got something decent to give us – we'll be over there around twelve-thirty.
	Secretary:	Yes Mr Simpson.

A management consultant with his clients

NOTES

12 **come up**: appear.
16 **clear the ground**: deal with general matters.
18 **fire away**: please start, go ahead.
23 **preliminary**: in preparation for the main matter.
24 **figure**: amount, sum.
29 **estimated**: what it is expected to be approximately.
33 **put in**: give, send in.
35 **draw up**: prepare.
39 **submitted**: sent in, handed in.
53 **sacking**: (colloquial): giving notice to, telling employees that they must leave their job, (Am) firing.
53 **up to you**: your responsibility, for you to decide.
63 **exhausted**: used up, come to the end of.
67 **files**: collection of papers arranged for convenient reference.
71 **canteen**: firm's own restaurant.
72 **decent**: reasonably good.

Practice

1 If possible, listen to the recording of the above dialogue, if not, two students read the parts of Simpson and the consultant. The rest of the class (books closed) must imagine they are Miss Honeyworths, and act as secretaries by taking notes in preparation for a written report to show to Simpson's superiors. Write the reports in indirect speech, so that it is possible to know who said what.

2 Rank said that the consultant's recommendations might lead to criticism and discontent among the company's staff. Why? What kind of recommendation might be particularly unpopular?

3 Make a list of all the shortened conversational forms (I'm, they've, etc.) used in this dialogue. Write the full form (I am, they have) alongside the shortened form.

9 The Manager and Change

The greatest of all problems for the manager is rapid change. The tempo of change has speeded up, hence the demands made on managers to plan for, and adjust to, changes are greater. All change requires both abilities. Some changes can be planned for in great detail, for instance, the switch to a new model. Others may be unforeseeable but, if the organization is kept sufficiently flexible, it will be able to cope with the unexpected. The number of completely unexpected changes can be kept to the minimum by foresight. Changes also mean adjustment. Without it the planning will be unsuccessful. The sources of major changes affecting management are:

(i) Innovations, which lead to new products and new methods of manufacture.
(ii) Shifts in market patterns as a result of innovations, of changes in consumer wants and of new methods of selling.
(iii) Greater competition, especially as a result of lower tariffs.
(iv) Changes in government regulations and taxation.
(v) New tools of management, such as the computer.
(iv) Changes in the background, training and occupation of those employed.

Let us now look at three of these to see what management can do to plan for them.

Innovations

The tempo of innovation is much greater than before, hence in some industries a company must spend heavily on research and development if it is to survive. To avoid stagnation or decline it must ever be on the look-out for new possibilities for growth. A study by the Stanford Research Institute of the causes of company growth in the U.S.A. reported findings which can also be helpful to British management. It found that the companies which had grown most, had the following characteristics:

a Early development of new, or rapidly growing, products and markets.

 b Organized programmes to seek and promote new business opportunities, for instance, long-range company planning, product research and development, market research, and the acquisition of other companies.
 c Proven competitive abilities in the company's present lines of business.
 d Courageous and energetic management which is willing to take carefully studied risks.
 e Good luck.

Changes in Consumer Expenditure

The pattern of consumer expenditure is changing rapidly. The age of marriage, the average number of children and how soon after marriage they are born, the proportion of women working, the level of education, the amount of leisure, and the availability of goods, all have changed in recent years and all influence what consumers buy and when. A major factor determining how money is spent is the standard of living and how it is distributed. There is a new market, for instance, created by the high earnings of teenagers who are spending heavily on leisure goods and services, such as pop records and dance-halls.

Changes in the Composition of the Working Force

Innovation, which is increasingly essential for many companies, will lead to a higher proportion of managers and specialists. The education, occupation and outlook of the people that managers will be working with, whether as subordinates or colleagues, is changing. Hence, as Peter Drucker suggested in an article entitled 'The Next Decade in Management' in 1959, 'Effective personnel management of the knowledge worker may require as much study as has been devoted in the past twenty-five years to the personnel management of the manual and clerical worker.'

[STEWART, R. *The Reality of Management*. Pan, 1967, pp. 163–171]

A consultant studies work in progress

NOTES

2 **tempo**: speed, rate.
2 **hence**: and therefore, consequently.
5 **switch**: change.
6 **unforeseeable**: that cannot be seen and planned for in advance.
7 **cope with**: successfully handle.
12 **innovations**: new ideas, inventions and models.
18 **computer**: 'electronic brain'. Also electronic data processing (EDP) and automatic data processing (ADP) machine.
37 **acquisition**: getting, acquiring, (often) buying.
38 **proven**: that has been proved.
57 **outlook**: way of looking at, thinking about things.
58 **subordinates**: those lower in rank, juniors. The opposite is *superiors*.
60 **decade**: ten years.
63 **manual worker**: one who works with his hands, 'blue-collar' worker.
63 **clerical worker**: one who does written work, clerk, 'white-collar' worker.

Practice

1 Give your own definitions of the meaning of the following as they are used in the above passage. Write your own definitions first, then look the words up to check their meaning.

speed up	major	decline
adjust	affect	finding
detail	want (noun)	courageous
flexible	tariff	availability
foresight	survive	composition
source	stagnation	devote

When you have checked your definition, put the words and expressions in sentences of your own.

2 A recent form of research used in business and other fields is called *value engineering*. The experts take an object and try to define exactly (a) what it is and (b) what it is for. For example, they may take as their object a *carpet*, and define it as *a kind of cloth, used to cover the floor*, or *to pick up dust*.

Now you try value engineering on the following:

a pop record	a newspaper
a manager	a cocktail party
taxation	a mill
a computer	an incentive
a company	a panel
a dance-hall	a queue
a canteen	a broom
a secretary	a can
a consultant	shorthand
a strike	loyalty

3 Teacher reads lines 1–42 at normal speed. Students take notes, then give oral reports on what they have heard. The reports can be recorded in the language laboratory if desired.

4 Give examples from your own country of shifts in market patterns caused by:

a innovations
b changes in consumer wants
c new methods of selling

5 To what extent is the computer used in your country? For what kind of tasks? What effects has it had on the speed with which various tasks can be performed? What effects on the number of staff employed?

6 Write an essay of 400–600 words on 'Changes in the Pattern of Consumer Expenditure in My Country'.

10 Executive Meeting

The effective meeting

The meeting, the report or the presentation are the typical work situations of the executive. They are his specific, everyday tools. They also make great demands on his time.

Effective executives ask themselves: 'Why are we having this meeting: do we want a decision, do we want to inform, or do we want to make clear to ourselves what we should be doing?' They will insist that the purpose be thought through and spelled out before a meeting is called, a report asked for, or a presentation organized. They insist that the meeting serve the contributions to which they have committed themselves.

The effective man always states at the outset of the meeting the specific purpose and contribution it is to achieve. He does not allow a meeting called to inform to degenerate into a discussion in which everyone has bright ideas. But a meeting called by him to stimulate thinking and ideas does not simply become a presentation on the part of one of the members, but is run to challenge and stimulate everybody in the room. He always, at the end of his meetings, goes back to the opening statement and relates the final conclusions to the original intent.

[DRUCKER, P. *The Effective Executive*. Heinemann, 1967]

Marmalade for Export?

Denton's Marmalade Ltd is contemplating going into the export market. Mr Lionel Denton, the Managing Director, has called in his Works Manager, Mr Leslie Bromley, and his Chief Accountant, Mrs Ruth Carmichael, to discuss the matter.

Denton: Good morning. I'm not going to make any speeches – we all know what we're here for, and what I'd like to hear are your ideas – purely off the record – about the whole question. Leslie?

Bromley: Well, I must admit I'm still a bit doubtful about this business. Exporting is always a tricky affair – costs a lot to get started, and you have to rely on outsiders – agents and so on – a lot. Wouldn't we be better to stick to the home market which we know and leave this export game to the other chaps?

Denton: H'm. You know, as I see it, there are big changes ahead – the country's going to be part of the EEC sooner or later – and any expanding firm that doesn't already have some experience and foothold in the export business is bound to be at a disadvantage. Ruth, how do you feel about this?

Carmichael: I'd like to say a word about the money side, Mr Denton. First, the Government is offering tax concessions to exporting firms. And second, I think Mr Bromley would agree that our potential capacity is already outgrowing the home market. The point is, can we afford to run at half speed?

Denton: Quite. So the idea is, we use the export market to take up the overflow from the home market.

Bromley: If I could just comment on Mrs Carmichael's first point for a moment. We've seen these Government concessions before – they're never very big and the politicians cut down on them just as soon as they're short of money.

Denton: You've got a point there. No good relying on official backing. This is a question we've got to decide ourselves, and never mind 'Export or Die' slogans and all that stuff.

Carmichael: It seems to me our first job is to find out just what it's likely to cost us to get started, and what kind of return we can expect over say the next two or three years.

Bromley: No harm in that. I'm not saying I'm against exporting per se, but –

Denton: Good. Well, that's about as far as we can go for now. Ruth, perhaps for the moment we can put you in charge of the 'export research project' – I think that's what they'd call it, isn't it? Meanwhile, perhaps it's time for a cup of coffee. Oh, by the way Leslie, about that new machinery you've ordered for B plant. . . .

NOTES

2 **presentation**: introducing or explaining of some matter.
8 **spelled out**: precisely explained.
10 **to which they have committed themselves**: which they have promised, engaged to do.
12 **outset**: beginning.
14 **degenerate**: become less effective.
17 **challenge**: bring out the fighting spirit.
17 **stimulate**: awaken, rouse.
20 **intent**: purpose.
23 **marmalade**: jam made from oranges or other citrus fruit.
24 **contemplating**: considering.
26 **Works Manager**: manager in charge of activities in the factory itself.
26 **Accountant**: a person whose profession is inspecting and auditing business accounts.
30 **off the record**: informal, unofficial.
33 **tricky**: difficult.
42 **bound to be**: sure to be.
45 **concessions**: reductions, allowances.
55 **cut down**: reduce.
58 **backing**: support.
62 **return**: profit.
64 **no harm in that**: there is nothing wrong with that.
65 **per se**: in itself.
71 **plant**: factory.

Practice

1 After the meeting, although he had said it was 'off the record', Mr Denton dictated what he remembered of the meeting on to a dictaphone, and got his secretary to type up what he had dictated later.

Listen to the recording of the dialogue, or set three students to read the parts of Denton, Bromley and Carmichael, while the rest of the class have their books shut. Then the rest of the class should divide up into pairs. One member of each pair is Mr Denton, the other is his secretary. The member playing Mr Denton should dictate what he can remember of the meeting; the secretary should then write up a report from what has been dictated. If tape-recorders are available, the dictations could be recorded to make the secretary's task easier and more realistic.

2 The class should be divided up into groups of 3-5, and each group hold an informal meeting along the lines of the dialogue above. One of each group should be designated the 'Director' and should lead the discussion. Subjects for discussion:

a Your firm is planning to put a new product on the market. What steps must the firm take to ensure its success? (Decide beforehand what kind of firm and what kind of new product).
b You wish to introduce a profit-sharing scheme into your firm. (One or more of the group should represent the firm's employees).
c You are planning a big publicity drive to sell a new product. Discuss the different kinds of publicity available and their relative suitability for your purpose. (Decide what kind of product beforehand.)

3 Did Mr Denton's meeting follow the lines laid down by Mrs Drucker for an 'effective meeting'? In what ways would you say his was a successful meeting? What were its weaknesses? In answering these questions ask yourself:

a Did Denton want a decision? If so, did he get one?
b Did he want to inform the others?
c Did he want to make clear to himself what the firm should be doing? If so, did he succeed?
d Did the meeting serve the purpose to which Denton had committed himself?
e Did Denton state the specific purpose and contribution the meeting was to achieve?
f Did the meeting degenerate?
g Did Denton go back to his opening statement at the end of the meeting and relate the final conclusions to it?

11 Conference English

Ever-increasing numbers of executives take part in various kinds of meetings where the main language is English. In order to participate successfully, the foreign business man needs not only to have a good grounding in commercial English, but also to be familiar with conference terminology. This article gives a number of the basic expressions needed for formal meetings.

Large meetings are usually called conferences. Such meetings are often held at regular intervals, though they may also be called for a special purpose. The delegates at conferences are often required to serve on committees, which are set up while the conference is in session. Delegates may also be asked to serve in an advisory capacity.

Preparing a Conference

A firm which acts as host for a conference will send out letters of invitation to delegates. If those invited cannot accept the invitation, they will write to say that they are unable to attend the meeting. The invitation will state the date when, and the place where, the meeting will be held. Often forms are sent out for delegates to fill in, or questionnaires.

Officers must be named for the conference, a programme of work drawn up and staff recruited. Those taking part will probably be paid an accommodation and subsistence allowance, and their travel expenses will be paid by their firm.

Before the conference it is important that rules of procedure are decided upon. A provisional agenda will be fixed, and a time-table drawn up. Documents should be in order. Official documents – such as contracts – are divided into chapters, sections, subsections or paragraphs, and subparagraphs. They may be provided with footnotes and appendices. Documents are first drawn up, then reproduced for distribution.

Officers of the Conference

The officers of a conference include a Chairman, probably a Vice-Chairman, and a Secretary who among other tasks keeps the

Anita–
one of our temporary staff

All good conference hotels need specialist staff from time to time. And the Grand at Brighton is an excellent conference hotel. Others we've hired have included a Highland piper in full regalia, several dozen conjurors, and a kangaroo.
Merely proving that if you want something special at a conference or a banquet, the Grand is a good place to go for it.
But all conferences at the Grand are special. Even without belly dancers. Things have a strange tendency to happen the way you want them to happen. And on time. Even unto the smallest detail.

Remarkable, perhaps. But not for the Grand. Or any other Express Hotel.
If you'd like to know the details, you can do two things.
Call Paul Boswell, the manager of the Grand. He'll tell you about the fabulous food and how nice Brighton is and how they've room for 400 delegates and six VIP suites and everything in communications from megaphones to scrambler phones.
On the other hand, we feel obliged to admit that there are eleven other Express conference hotels with a very similar outlook.

Our man George Robertson in London will tell you all about them. (Or more about the Grand if it keeps down the phone bill.) So remember. Express Hotels are the ones to go for. George Robertson the man to contact.

LONDON: Bailey's, Berners and Brent Bridge Hotels. SEASIDE: The Grand and the Royal, Scarborough. Warnes, Worthing. Marsham Ct., Bournemouth. The Grand, Brighton. Queens, Eastbourne. COUNTRY: Royal Clarence, Exeter. The Bull, Gerrards Cross, and The Viking, York.

EXPRESS CONFERENCE HOTELS COVER THE COUNTRY

Our man
George Robertson
Sales Promotion Officer

Our man
Paul Boswell
Manager
of the Grand
Brighton

Express Hotels
Courtfield Close, Courtfield Road, London SW7 Tel: 01-370 4121 Telex: 916733

minutes at meetings. The host firm of the conference may provide a typewriting service, mimeographing facilities, and an information desk near the conference hall.

When the conference is in session, the Chairman will open the meeting. He may declare the discussion open, or he may call upon a certain speaker who has been asked to make a speech. While others are speaking, it is the Chairman's duty to keep the meeting in order, he may for instance need to request delegates to keep to the point under discussion, or invite speakers to be brief. The Chairman's ruling on a point of order is normally accepted as final.

The Debate

Those wishing to speak may put their names on the list of speakers, or indicate their desire to intervene in a debate by saying to the Chairman, 'Mr Chairman, I ask to speak.' A speaker may address the meeting from his place, or go up to the rostrum. A delegate may express agreement with the previous speaker, or raise an objection to what another speaker has said. This objection may be sustained or overruled by the Chairman.

During the debate a number of motions may be put forward. Before these can be voted upon, they must be seconded. Delegates may vote for or against a motion or abstain from voting. For a motion to be adopted it must be supported by the requisite majority. If everyone is in favour of the motion, it is carried unanimously, and a resolution is passed. Voting may be carried out by secret ballot, or the Chairman may simply say, 'Please signify by show of hands'. Voting is performed in the same way for a candidate who agrees to stand for election to a particular office at the conference.

At the end of a session, the Chairman closes the debate, and adjourns the meeting. At the end of the conference, he will probably make a closing speech, and some delegate will propose a vote of thanks for the host firm.

In conclusion, for those who are particularly in need of Conference English, there is an excellent glossary in English, French, Spanish, Russian, Italian and German, called *Conference Terminology* (Elsevier, 1962), which has been of considerable assistance in compiling this article. Further material can also be found in Chapters 12 and 22 of this book.

CONFERENCE NOTES

- 7 **conference**: also congress, convention (Am).
- 11 **in session**: taking place.
- 22 **accommodation**: place to live in, e.g. a hotel room.
- 22 **subsistence**: food and drink.
- 25 **provisional**: temporary, for the time being.
- 25 **agenda**: list of matters to be dealt with.
- 25 **time-table**: schedule (Am).
- 29 **footnotes**: notes printed at the bottom of the page.
- 29 **appendices**: singular: appendix. Additional material put at the end of a document.
- 33 **Secretary**: also *Clerk*.
- 34 **minutes**: written record of what is said and done at a meeting.
- 35 **mimeographing**: reproducing by special process in many copies.
- 43 **point of order**: matter of correct procedure.
- 46 **intervene**: interrupt, speak in between other speakers.
- 47 **Mr Chairman**: a lady is addressed as Madam Chairman.
- 47 **I ask to speak**: I ask for the floor (Am).
- 47 **address the meeting**: take the floor (Am).
- 48 **rostrum**: platform for public speaking.
- 51 **sustained**: supported.
- 51 **overruled**: not allowed.
- 52 **motions**: also proposals.
- 53 **seconded**: supported by a second person.
- 54 **abstain from voting**: not vote.
- 55 **adopted**: also carried.
- 55 **requisite**: necessary, required.
- 57 **resolution**: formal determination.
- 57 **ballot**: ticket, paper, etc. used in voting.
- 58 **signify**: show how you wish to vote.
- 60 **office**: position of duty, trust or authority.
- 62 **adjourns**: suspends until a later time.

Practice

1 Give your own definitions of the meaning of the following as they are used in the above passage. Write your own definitions first, then look up the words to check their meaning.

executive	draw up	put forward
participate	in order	vote
grounding	reproduce	adopt
terminology	distribution	unanimously
to set up	to request	procedure
advisory	brief	candidate
attend	to address	stand for

When you have checked your definitions, put the words and expressions in sentences of your own.

2 Fill in the article (the, a, an) where necessary:

a For ... motion to be passed it must be supported by ... requisite majority.

b ... firm which acts as ... host for ... conference will send out ... letters of ... invitation to ... delegates.

c ... documents are first drawn up, then reproduced for ... distribution.

d At ... end ... session, ... Chairman closes ... debate.

e ... speaker may address ... meeting from his place, or go up to ... rostrum.

f ... officers of ... conference include ... Secretary who among ... other tasks keeps ... minutes at ... meetings.

g It is ... Chairman's duty to keep ... meeting in ... order.

h ... foreign business man needs to have ... good grounding in ... commercial terminology.

3 Make a list of all the words and expressions in this passage which you think belong specifically to conference terminology. Compare your list with the Conference Notes at the end of the passage. Make sure you know the meaning of any terms in your list not included in the Notes.

4 You are the representative of a firm acting as host for a conference on 'Paper in a Changing World'. Write a letter of invitation to Mr Martin Dean, Managing Director of British Pulp and Paper, Ltd.

5 You are Mr Dean. Write a letter in reply to the above invitation, *a* accepting, *b* refusing the invitation.

12 At a Conference

David Simpson is attending a conference at Brighton. The theme of the conference is 'Translation for the Business World'.

Chairman: Ladies and gentlemen, now that we have heard the main speakers, I declare the discussion open.
Brand: Mr Chairman, I ask for the floor.
Chairman: Yes, Mr Brand.
Brand: Mr Chairman, I just wish to say that in my capacity of export manager in a large U.S. corporation exporting all over the world, I have found that it is always best where possible to use one's own translators.
Lovelace: Mr Chairman, I ask to speak.
Chairman: Yes, Mrs – er ——
Lovelace: Miss Lovelace. Mr Chairman, I'm sure what the last speaker says is very true, but my experience as a translator is that very few companies, at any rate in this country, are willing to take on translators as permanent staff at a decent salary. I remember in 1956 – or was it '57? – trying to get a job of this kind, and I must have applied to half a dozen firms, but none of them showed the slightest ——
Chairman: Thank you Miss Lovelace, but I'm afraid we're straying a little from the point under discussion. If I may just remind the meeting, our subject today is 'How can we train good translators?'
Simpson: Mr Chairman, I ——
Chairman: Yes. Mr – er – Simpson, isn't it?
Simpson: That's right. Mr Chairman. I must confess that I'm rather new in this field, but it has struck me that a commercial translator must need a good deal of commercial experience, which he – or she – is unlikely to get unless he works in a commercial firm.
Brand: Right. That's just my point. I ——
Chairman: Mr Brand, I must remind you that all remarks should be addressed to the Chair.
Brand: I apologize Mr Chairman. – May I go on?

Chairman: Yes, but please be brief – there are several other delegates who have indicated that they wish to speak.
Brand: Thank you. Well, Mr Chairman, as I was about to say, I believe that a business translator should have both a sound linguistic and business training in the first place, and he should then be permanently employed by the corporation for whom he translates.
Chairman: Mr Simpson
Simpson: Mr Chairman, I should like to ask whether any research work has been done to discover what in fact is the background of the translators used at present, and to what extent they are on the permanent staff of the firms that use them?
Chairman: Can anyone help us on this point? – No? – Well, this seems to be a question which should be resolved before we can go into our subject more deeply. Perhaps we should form a committee to look into it.
Simpson: I propose that Miss Lovelace should be on the committee.
Brand: I second that.
Chairman: Any more proposals? – Well, could I suggest that perhaps Mr Brand and Mr Simpson might serve on the committee also?
Voice: I second Mr Brand.
Voice: I second Mr Simpson.
Simpson: Mr Chairman. I appreciate the honour, but I regret that I have to leave the conference tomorrow, so I am obliged reluctantly to refuse to serve on the committee.
Chairman: I think our committee should consist of at least three members, so could I please have another nomination.
Voice: I propose Mr Fields.
Voice: Seconded.
Chairman: Thank you. If there are no further nominations, it will be unnecessary to take a vote. And now I see it is just five o'clock, so I declare the meeting adjourned until tomorrow at 10 a.m.

NOTES

1 **theme**: subject.
7 **in my capacity of**: while acting as.
17 **decent**: reasonably good.
21 **straying**: wandering away from, not keeping to the point.
34 **addressed to the Chair**: spoken to the Chairman: in other words Brand should have begun his remark with 'Mr Chairman'.
40 **sound**: thorough, reliable.
50 **resolved**: to which an answer should be found.
51 **go into**: examine.
52 **look into**: examine, go into.
63 **reluctantly**: unwillingly.
65 **nomination**: proposal of a candidate.

Practice

1 You are Secretary of the conference meeting above. Listen to the recording of the meeting, or get students to read it. The class keeps the minutes of the meeting. Here are some notes on minutes:

The outline for minutes can most easily be obtained from the agenda of the meeting. The agenda for this meeting (drawn up by the Chairman and the Secretary) was:

1 Reading of minutes of last meeting
2 General subject of meeting
3 Speeches by: ...
4 General discussion
5 Any other business
6 Next meeting

Items in the minutes should be numbered and given headings, e.g.:

1 Minutes
2 Subject of meeting
3 Speakers
4 Discussion
5 Nomination of committee
6 Next meeting

Under 1 the place and date of the meeting can de included, e.g. 'The minutes of the ... meeting held at ... on ... read and approved.'

Minutes are not the same as a report: they are briefer and deal with facts, not opinions. Therefore the names of the speakers and their subjects (you can invent these) will be sufficient under 3. Also only the names of those who took part in the discussion and mention of what matters were discussed will suffice under 4.

Under 5 mention the purpose of the committee and the members nominated. Since this was a resolution, begin:

'*Resolved*: that a committee should be formed for the purpose of ..., consisting of the following members: ...'

For further information about minutes, see for example MARTIN BUCKNALL G. *How to Take Minutes*. Pitman, 1967.

2 A formal meeting. Choose a Chairman to lead the meeting, a Secretary to keep the minutes, and two or three official speakers to introduce the subject under discussion. Remember to observe the rules and use the correct forms as given in the last two chapters. Some suggested subjects for the meeting:

a The Need for Learning Foreign Languages in Business
b Change in the Executive World
c The Need for More and Better Advertising
d How to Export Better

3 Did the Chairman handle the meeting well, *a* in the above piece, *b* in your classroom? What would you say were his strong and weak points?

4 What word was Miss Lovelace going to use when the Chairman interrupted her (line 21)?

5 Complete Mr Brand's interrupted sentence on line 32 ('I ...')

6 Mr Brand used one or two American terms that differ from the British ones. What were they?

7 Were Miss Lovelace and Mr Brand good choices for the committee? Give reasons for your answers.

Part II
Manufacturer to Consumer

13 Export Services

London Venue for World's Exporters
Exhibition and Conference on Export Services

Long before Napoleon Bonaparte described the British as 'a nation of shopkeepers', they had been trading regularly with all parts of the world; but in international marketing nothing stands still, and everyone engaged in this field must continually develop new methods to meet changing circumstances. Recognition of the important role export services play has led in Britain to an annual Export Services Exhibition.

The companies and organizations represented cover such activities as shipping and airfreight services, the provision of finance and credit, packaging and materials handling, export printing, and language translation.

Packing services for successful exporting

However good a product may be, it will fail to achieve repeat orders unless it reaches the consumer in good condition and on the due delivery date. Although the manufacturer may have encased the product in an attractive protective pack and have made certain that it leaves the factory in good time, damage or delay may occur during the intervals of time and space that separate the producer and his overseas customers.

During this all-important intermediate stage, goods in transit are in the hands of a country's 'export services', which pack, handle and transport them by the most convenient means to their eventual destination.

Specialist Packing

As the problems of packing goods for export become more complex, there is a tendency for manufacturers to hand over this function to specialist packers. There are many such firms in Britain, which offer a service related to the customer's needs. If a comprehensive service is needed, a firm will collect the goods from the manufacturer's factory in its own transport; convey them to its

The big market.

The USA–biggest, most booming market in the world. And TWA flies you there. Comprehensively –we cover far more cities in the USA–39 of them– than any other transatlantic airline. Advantageously –low off season fares are in effect right now, and so are big internal fare discounts. Expertly–in London we have more people, knowing more about the USA, than any other airline. (And we've just opened the World Travel Centre on Park Avenue in New York–with staff ready to deal with any travel problem you care to present.)

Your Travel Agent knows all about TWA. Call him soon–it could turn out to be a highly profitable conversation.

London: 01-636 4090 • *Manchester:* 061-834 7853
Birmingham: 021-236 0191 • *Glasgow:* 041-332 1548

*Service mark owned exclusively by Trans World Airlines, Inc.

central packing area; and afterwards deliver them to docks or airport for shipment to the country of destination.

35 The increasing complexity of many foreign trading regulations and practices is making it more and more difficult for manufacturers, especially the small or medium-size concern, to undertake directly the function of shipping goods overseas. The specialist organizations therefore offer not only facilities for physical handling of the goods,
40 from the maker's dispatch bay to overseas destinations, but also the arrangement of shipping space and documentation associated with insurance, freight rates and all export and import regulations.

Containerization explosion

There is no doubt that the whole concept of the shipment of goods
45 has been changed by the technique of containerization, the scheme under which standard containers, internationally agreed as to dimensions, weight, structural strength, slinging positions and other features, are loaded at a given marshalling point and taken from there to their destination, without breaking bulk, in standard
50 transport. By itself, the idea of putting goods into a special container for shipment by land, sea or air is not new; what is novel is the concept of a container *system*, under which a standardized container (accepted both nationally and internationally) is considered as part of an integrated handling system that includes movement from the
55 factory by standardized transport; handling at the docks by a standard system on to specially designed and equipped ships; and suitable off-loading and handling facilities at the other end.

Special problems of airfreight

Transport of suitable freight by air is bound to rise rapidly over
60 the next few years, as bigger and speedier air freighters, specially equipped to handle containerized loads, come into service.

Airfreight offers speed and saving on packing costs for goods that are light in weight and occupy little space in relation to their value; the rising trend in airfreight, which has been evident for some time,
65 has still by no means reached its peak. One problem in this field (which applies to containerization generally) is the selection of a procedure for assembling the individual items of freight, often from many sources, into a large enough 'package' to fill a container. The

specialist organization, with its facilities and expertise, can maintain a central collecting point where individual consignments, brought in from a wide area, are grouped into container loads for particular destinations.

In conclusion

Throughout the Exhibition, the emphasis is on assisting the flow of exports everywhere, because it is only by increasing the flow of goods and services across *all* frontiers that the world can raise its living standards to the level everyone desires.

[FORD E. 'London Venue for World's Exporters'. *International Trade Forum*, September 1967]

NOTES

- 1 **venue**: meeting-place.
- 7 **recognition**: acknowledgement, noticing and applauding of what has been achieved.
- 11 **airfreight**: transporting goods by air.
- 11 **provision**: offering, providing.
- 12 **credit**: permission to pay later.
- 15 **repeat orders**: more orders of the same kind.
- 17 **due . . . date**: the fixed, agreed time.
- 17 **encased**: put into, wrapped, covered (with).
- 19 **in good time**: not late, not at the last minute, with time to spare.
- 22 **in transit**: while being transported.
- 30 **comprehensive**: covering the whole field.
- 32 **transport**: transport vehicles.
- 40 **dispatch bay**: part of factory, etc. from which goods are sent.
- 41 **documentation**: the various documents needed.
- 42 **rates**: costs, prices.
- 43 **explosion**: sudden increase in use.
- 47 **slinging positions**: points for fastening ropes or chains used in handling freight.
- 48 **given**: certain, arranged.
- 48 **marshalling point**: place where goods, etc. are brought together, collecting point. (see lines 70–72.)

49 **breaking bulk**: dividing up large items into smaller parts.
54 **integrated**: where parts are combined into a whole.
57 **off-loading**: unloading, discharging.
59 **bound**: sure.
60 **air freighters**: airplanes for carrying freight.
69 **expertise** expert knowledge, know-how.

Practice

1 Give your own definitions of the meaning of the following as they are used in the above passage. Write your own definitions first, then look the words up to check their meaning.

be engaged in	convenient	facilities
play a role	eventual	dimensions
handling	destination	novel
fail	tendency	standardized
protective	convey	trend
delay	complexity	reach its peak
intermediate	concern	assemble

When you have checked your definitions, put the words and expressions in sentences of your own.

2 Give opposites to the following:

long before	attractive	novel
regularly	in good time	loading
nothing	to separate	rapidly
stand still	convenient	suitable
continually	eventual	light in weight
changing	complexity	rising
important	there is no doubt	assisting
successful	standard	increasing
fail	a given point	everyone

3 The teacher reads about thirty lines of the passage at normal speed, while students take notes on what is read. They are given a few minutes to look through their notes, and then asked to give oral reports. This exercise can also be done in the language laboratory, with students recording their reports.

4 Answer these questions orally:

a What are the export services mentioned in this passage?
b What are the functions of specialist packers?
c What is containerization? What are its advantages?
d What are the advantages of airfreight? Disadvantages?

5 Question for discussion. What export services are available in your country? What further services do you think would be desirable?

14 Land, Sea and Air

Announcer: This is B.B.C., Radio Four. Tonight, Mary Owen has brought to the third 'Business World' programme Mr George Baker, who has been dealing with transport problems for many years.

Owen: I'd like to know, Mr Baker, whether you think airfreight is taking over from other methods of transporting goods.

Baker: It's certainly becoming more and more popular, but on the other hand the need for all kinds of transport is also growing.

Owen: I suppose the main advantage of airfreight is speed.

Baker: Yes, although there is one snag there – air space is in such demand that it often has to be booked a very long time in advance.

Owen: So in some cases it may be easier to send the goods by sea.

Baker: Easier and cheaper.

Owen: What other factors should be considered when sending goods overseas?

Baker: It's an advantage to have an airfield or a good port near the final destination of the goods.

Owen: What constitutes a good port?

Baker: Well, for instance the harbour should be easy of access and should offer good mooring-space.

Owen: And then you'll need good facilities and equipment for loading and discharging cargoes I imagine.

Baker: Yes, there must be an adequate supply of dockers, machinery like cranes, sheds for storing goods and so on.

Owen: Yes, I can understand warehousing must be a major problem. Then I suppose there are various organizational tasks that must be looked after.

Baker: Yes, a good port must have forwarding facilities and ship-brokers to arrange for the chartering of boats.

Owen: Modern shipping is certainly a complex business. But we haven't said anything about land transport yet.

The perfect match

(Containerisation & Aluminium)

Aluminium is strong. It resists impact — essential for containers that are always on the move from one form of transport to another. Its lightness reduces container deadweight and increases profit making payload. Its naturally durable surface minimises maintenance costs. It also has a high recovery value.

The British Aluminium Company can offer a full range of products required for containers:
* Baco Aluminium sheet (plain and pre-painted).
* Extrusions.
* 8′ wide coil for seamless roofs.
* Reefer Flooring for refrigerated containers.

For further information contact:
>Containers–Extension 222
>The British Aluminium Company Ltd
>Norfolk House, St. James's Square
>London SW1. Tel: 01-839 8888

80% of American containers are made in aluminium. You can't ignore that much experience.

BACO ALUMINIUM FOR CONTAINERS

The British Aluminium Company Ltd

	Baker:	No. Well, road and rail transport are of course generally complementary services to transport by sea and air.
40	*Owen:*	What about big trucks that go from country to country in Europe?
	Baker:	You're quite right, I was forgetting those.
	Owen:	They're very versatile, aren't they?
	Baker:	Yes – for instance they often run these trucks right on to car ferries without removing the load at all.
45	*Owen:*	I've heard the railways are feeling the pressure badly from road haulage competition.
	Baker:	Yes. One reason is that road transport is so much more flexible.
50	*Owen:*	Now Mr Baker, is there anything about the future of long-distance freighting you'd like to mention?
	Baker:	Only this, that I believe the containerization explosion will continue to expand rapidly for some years to come.
	Owen:	Thank you very much Mr Baker.
	Announcer:	You have been listening to . . . .

NOTES

12 **snag**: difficulty.
12 **space**: room in which to transport goods.
21 **destination**: place to which goods are sent.
23 **easy of access**: easy to enter.
24 **mooring-space**: place where ships can be anchored or tied up while in harbour.
26 **discharging**: unloading.
27 **dockers**: those who load and unload the ship; also dock worker, (Am) longshoreman.
28 **cranes**: machines for lifting goods, e.g. on and off ships.
33 **forwarding**: looking after transport, sending on to somewhere else.
34 **ship-brokers**: firms that represent shipping companies and arrange such matters as mooring-space, payment of pilot and harbour dues, etc. Also *ship's agent*.
34 **chartering**: hiring (of ships).
38 **complementary**: additional, auxiliary.
42 **versatile**: many-sided.
44 **car ferries**: ships specially designed for carrying cars.
46 **road haulage**: road transport.

Practice

1 Make sentences beginning or ending with the following:

    I suppose   I believe   I imagine
    I should think   I hear   I expect
    I see   I understand I bet

2 Re-tell the above dialogue in indirect speech.

3 What were Mr Baker's opinions about airfreighting? How did they compare with the opinions put forward in the previous chapter?

4 What constitutes a good port according to Mr Baker? What other requirements can you think of?

5 What is the situation regarding rail and road transport in your country?

15 Packaging – An Under-rated Technique

A Summary of the Development and Application of Packaging Techniques

Some years ago, after the Malaysian Government drew up a programme for extending the television network, Western manufacturers of TV sets became interested in this market. Many of them were bitterly disappointed. The equipment was arriving damaged either by humidity or by unloading. Handling by Malaysian dockers caused a loss rate of almost fifty per cent. In addition, the rather neutral colour of the sets was considered too dull by customers who are often more sensitive to colour than to technical and commercial advantages.

Japan captured almost two-thirds of the Malaysian market. Out of 5,000 sets sold in 1963, 3,800 were of Japanese origin. The reason for their success: Japanese manufacturers not only had adapted the external appearance of their sets to the exotic tastes of the Malaysian market, but had also made a thorough study of the problems of packaging and damp-resistance, and of the hazards of unloading, forwarding and transport over country roads.

By packing the sets in large containers requiring mechanical handling, it was possible to avoid the shortcomings of individual handling formerly carried out by unskilled workers.

Of course, the quality of the packaging alone did not account for the success of Japanese television sets in the Malaysian market – price differences and geographical advantages also played a part. But in this instance, packaging, to which exporters all too often fail to pay sufficient attention, was able to demonstrate that it had become an essential tool in competing for external markets. Economies on packaging prove very expensive in the end.

Traditional characteristics

Packaging techniques vary according to the nature of the goods and the climatic conditions.

The main functions of efficient packaging are:
a to protect the product;

HOW TO SAVE SPACE

The square shaped bottle of
Johnnie Walker will fit into the corner
of any cupboard. Try it.
 It won't actually stay there for long
but you can always buy another one.

b to facilitate transport;
c to promote sales.

The publicity value of packaging is generally recognized, as is its functional utility. What is termed 'non-returnable packaging' could in many cases be called 'dual-purpose packaging' – for example, mustard jars that can be used as drinking glasses, or aluminium containers that can be converted into bath tubs or basins. The sales value of a good product is certainly not limited to its basic qualities, but also includes its external presentation – the packaging.

'The package sells the product'

One of the features of the present trend in packaging techniques is the advertising aspect.

Many articles have been published in specialized magazines on the phenomenon that partly accounts for the growth in consumption: namely, 'the package sells the product'.

In the United States, where the science of 'motivation' is most developed, it has been estimated that almost eighty per cent of purchasing decisions in supermarkets are a matter of impulse-buying. One can readily understand why so much attention is paid to the attractiveness of packaging for major consumer products.

Conclusion

In most developed countries the packaging industry shows trends with the same economic and technological characteristics. The quality of the packaging and the presentation is increasingly becoming a valuable sales argument. But the efforts should not become the privilege of industrial countries only.

Some developing countries have grasped the importance of packaging for the sale of their primary products to the large consumer markets. Today, with increasing interdependence of national economies and growing competition for geographical areas, no country can permit itself to disregard economic developments in any part of the world.

[BOISSY P. 'Packaging – an Underrated Technique'. *International Trade Forum*, November 1965]

NOTES

title **under-rated**: under-valued.
 1 **application**: ways of using.
 3 **drew up**: prepared.
 6 **bitterly**: deeply, very.
 7 **humidity**: dampness, moisture.
 8 **dockers**: dock workers.
 8 **rate**: proportion.
 9 **neutral**: quiet, having no definite characteristics.
 9 **dull**: uninteresting, not bright.
15 **exotic**: strikingly unusual.
17 **damp-resistance**: preventing the goods from suffering from damp.
17 **hazards**: dangers.
20 **shortcomings**: disadvantages.
21 **formerly**: before.
28 **economies**: saving.
37 **non-returnable**: that cannot be returned.
38 **dual-purpose**: that can have two uses.
39 **jar**: glass container.
42 **external presentation**: what the product (and its covering) looks like when the customer gets it.
50 **motivation**: the reason why people act in a certain way.
52 **impulse-buying**: buying something when you see it, without having previously decided to buy it.
59 **sales argument**: reason why the customer should buy the product.
61 **grasped**: understood.
65 **disregard**: take no notice of.

Practice

1 Give your own definition of the meaning of the following as they are used in the above passage. Write your own definitions first, then look the words up to check their meaning.

extend	tool	capture the market
disappoint	facilitate	publicity
to damage	promote sales	origin
convert	adapt	stimulus
demonstrate	invention	essential
trend	economic	to grasp

When you have checked your definitions, put the words and expressions in sentences of your own.

2 Value engineering. Try to define exactly, *a* what the following are, and *b* what they are for.

a television set	a car ferry	a salary
a docker	a ship-broker	a rostrum
a container	a crane	a footnote
packaging	a warehouse	a debate
mustard	a translation	voting
a jar	a conference	minutes of a meeting
a bath tub	a chairman	

3 Answer the following orally:

a How did the Japanese capture the Malaysian TV market?
b What are the main functions of packaging?
c Give examples of 'dual-purpose' packaging.
d How can packaging advertise the product?
e Do you consider that packaging techniques are highly developed in your country? Give reasons for your answer.

4 Write an essay of 400–600 words on 'The Importance of Efficient Packaging'.

16 Talking about Packaging Materials

In his new job of Export Manager, David Simpson is trying to collect information about every branch of the export business. Now he is talking to Brian Baldwin, an expert on packaging materials.

Simpson: Well, Mr Baldwin, I wonder if you could tell me a bit about the various kinds of packaging materials on the market.
Baldwin: All right. As you probably know, materials like paperboard, wood, jute and metals have held the field for quite a time.
Simpson: What about plastics?
Baldwin: They're a relatively new arrival in the field, but they've come on the market in a big way.
Simpson: Then there've been changes in packaging techniques too I suppose.
Baldwin: Certainly. Take the aerosol packs for example, they're used an enormous lot nowadays.
Simpson: I'm in the canned foods line myself as you know. Have there been any outstanding advances in the foodstuffs field lately?
Baldwin: The biggest innovations have been in vacuum-pack techniques and cold-storage processes.
Simpson: Then, can you tell me anything about the relative popularity of different kinds of packaging materials?
Baldwin: Well, the leader is paperboard – it accounts for around half the market.
Simpson: That's used for packages of all sizes of course.
Baldwin: Quite. Then there are metals, glass, plastics and wood.
Simpson: The overall consumption of packaging materials must be terrific.
Baldwin: It is, and it's constantly on the increase.
Simpson: I suppose one reason for that is the growing use of non-returnable packaging.
Baldwin: Yes – in France for instance they've even tried to do away with the traditional glass wine bottles and replace them with non-returnable plastic containers.

Simpson: I should think they've got a job on there.

Baldwin: Yes, people can be very conservative about some things.

Simpson: Coming back to the materials, why is paperboard so popular?

Baldwin: Well, it's got quite a few qualities which give it advantages over competing materials. It's flexible and strong, cheap, adaptable ——

Simpson: Heavens – you ought to be selling paperboard, you make it sound like the best product ever marketed.

Baldwin: – And it's easily disposable, so it's ideal for non-returnable packaging.

Simpson: Well, thank you very much indeed – I won't bother you any more now, but I wonder if I could contact you again if I run into any specific problems in this line where I need some expert outside advice?

Baldwin: I'll be glad to help any time I can.

Simpson: Oh yes, and would you just drop a note into our office about your consulting fee.

Baldwin: Thanks, I'll do that.

NOTES

8 **jute**: strong fibre used for making fabrics, ropes, etc.

8 **held the field**: been the chief materials used in packaging.

15 **aerosol**: spray-type container.

28 **overall**: total.

36 **they've got a job**: (colloquial) they are faced with a difficult task.

41 **flexible**: can be bent without breaking.

42 **adaptable**: can be used for different purposes.

45 **easily disposable**: easily destroyed, got rid of.

50 **outside**: from someone not actually working for the firm.

53 **consulting**: giving advice.

Practice

1 Although she did not say anything, David Simpson's faithful secretary, Victoria Honeyworth, was making notes all the time that Simpson and Baldwin were talking. Listen to the recording, or get

two students to read the dialogue, while the rest of the class act as Honeyworths and take notes on what they read, in preparation for writing a short report.

2 Ask the expert. The class is divided into pairs. One of the pair wishes to obtain advice like David Simpson, the other is the expert. This exercise is best given as homework so that the one who wishes for advice can prepare questions and the expert can absorb information about his subject. Some suggested subjects:

a packaging methods
b airfreighting
c specialist packing
d conference technique
e uses of PR
f what to look for in a secretary
g export developments in Ireland
h how to select an export market
i import regulations in your own country
j marketing in the Middle East.

Some information or ideas can be found in Book 1 and the earlier chapters of this book concerning all these subjects.

17 Hong Kong: Distribution Center

Of all freeport distribution centers in the world today, Hong Kong is certainly the most glamorous. The combination of this Oriental city's geography and the absence of import taxes has long made Hong Kong the ideal storehouse for transit goods to and from Asia.

There is one railroad in the colony; two freight trains a day were scheduled while I was there. Hong Kong can boast about 700 miles of road, with about 12,000 registered trucks. Kai Tak International Airport is efficient as well as beautiful, with an 8,340-foot runway, extending into the harbor area, which can safely handle today's biggest jets. As a result, a steadily increasing percentage of international freight is being carried by air. This growth is expected to increase sharply in the next few years.

Busy Harbor

For the present, however, Hong Kong depends on its world-famous harbor for most of its shipments. It's a busy place. Some seventy per cent of the cargoes are still loaded or unloaded by sampans or lighters. Despite this primitive method of cargo handling, Hong Kong is reputed to have the fastest turnaround time of any port in the Far East.

I was told that the Marine Department maintains some fifty-two moorings for ocean-going vessels. The commercial wharves can accommodate vessels up to 750 feet long with a draft up to 32 feet. All are equipped with modern cargo-handling equipment.

There are four large wharf and warehouse companies and over a hundred small ones. These provide ample facilities for the off-loading and storage of all kinds of cargoes. Total storage capacity is estimated at over forty million cubic feet.

After touring the harbor, I made my way to the largest of these companies. Traffic Manager D. R. Bland had promised to show me round and answer some of my questions.

Lighter problems

Bland had just finished a memorandum on the very subject I brought up – the clutter of lighters in the harbor. He confirmed that this was indeed a problem.

'It's cheap enough for the shipper from Hong Kong,' said Bland, 'but it causes many problems for buyers and consignees at destination. This is what happens:

'1 Knowing the ship's name and sailing date, manufacturers wait until the last minute before placing their goods in the sampans. These craft all arrive alongside on the final day of loading.

'2 Loading is carried out piecemeal from numerous small craft each carrying mixed consignments. Often single consignments are split between two or more craft.

'3 Unloading at the port of discharge follows the pattern of loading. Goods are landed badly mixed and often damaged.

'4 Difficulties are caused in sorting. This involves time and increases costs. These costs, mainly labor expenses, are much higher than those here in Hong Kong.'

Shipment Consolidation

Bland pointed out that the solution obviously lay in consolidation of shipments. 'We're already doing this successfully,' he said, 'on behalf of a large chain store with 1,120 retail outlets in one European country. Orders are placed with Hong Kong manufacturers for these stores. The order consists of many different sizes, hardware items, toys and the like. These are allocated to each store according to individual requirements. The merchandise is delivered to our warehouse, where expert personnel sort out each package and apply a label bearing the code number of the store, and a color mark denoting the railway regional area in which the particular store is located.

'All goods are then consolidated so that all packages for a particular rail regional area are brought together in sub units. Then the sub units are consolidated to provide one block of cargo stowed in the vessel under one B/L. On arrival at the port of discharge, packages are assembled by color mark and put in rail cars for each regional area. When the rail cars arrive at destination, all goods for each particular store are put onto waiting trucks for dispatch without delay.'

With Mao's Permission

Hong Kong, of course, has the added problem that it can only continue to exist as long as Red China permits. Yet the colony continues to flourish, to manufacture, to import and to export. As long as it does, there will continue to be a market for U.S. goods, and a need to contribute to this Asian *entrepôt*.

['Hong Kong'. *Distribution Manager*, October 1967]

NOTES

General note: This article is written by an American, and consequently there are some differences of spelling (harbor, harbour) from the general British spelling in this book. Where there are differences of meaning or usage, these have been noted.

- 1 **freeport**: port not included in customs territory so as to expedite trans-shipment.
- 4 **transit**: on the way from one place to another.
- 5 **railroad**: (Br) railway.
- 5 **freight train**: (Br) goods train.
- 7 **truck**: (Br) (often) lorry.
- 16 **sampan**: small, Oriental boat.
- 17 **lighter**: vessel used for unloading (lightening) or loading ships.
- 18 **turnaround time**: time from when the ship arrives until it leaves the port.
- 21 **moorings**: places where the ship can be fastened (moored) either alongside the quay or near the shore.
- 21 **wharves**: singular: wharf. Structure alongside which ship can be moored for loading, etc.
- 22 **accommodate**: have room for.
- 22 **draft**: depth.
- 25 **ample facilities**: plenty of opportunity.
- 32 **memorandum**: report.
- 33 **clutter**: disorderly confusion.
- 36 **consignees**: those to whom the goods are sent (consigned).
- 40 **craft**: boats, vessels.
- 41 **piecemeal**: piece by piece.
- 46 **sorting**: arranging, separating according to sort.
- 49 **consolidation**: bringing together into larger units.
- 54 **hardware**: metalware, such as tools, locks, knives, etc.
- 55 **allocated**: set apart for a particular purpose, assigned, allotted.
- 57 **apply**: put on.
- 59 **denoting**: showing.
- 63 **sub units**: smaller units, parts of larger units.
- 63 **stowed**: placed in the ship.

64 **B/L**: bill of lading. Receipt for goods placed on board a vessel.
64 **discharge**: unloading.
74 **entrepôt**: commercial centre to which goods are sent for distribution.

Practice

1 Give your own definitions of the meaning of the following as they are used in the above passage. Write your own definitions first, then look the words up to check their meaning.

glamorous	storage	chain store
combination	capacity	retail
absence	confirm	hardware
scheduled	alongside	merchandise
registered	split	label
cargo	involve	dispatch
reputed	solution	flourish
maintain	on behalf of	contribute

When you have checked your definitions, put the words and expressions in sentences of your own.

2 Substitute other words for the words in italics, e.g.:
Hong Kong has the *further* problem that it can only continue to exist as long as Red China *allows*.
With substitutions:
Hong Kong has the *added* problem that it can only continue to exist as long as Red China *permits*.
Do this exercise without looking at the passage, then check your results afterwards.

a The *lack* of import taxes has long made Hong Kong the *perfect* storehouse for transit goods.
b A steadily *growing* percentage of international freight is being *transported* by air.
c Hong Kong is *said* to have the *most rapid* turnaround time in the Far East.
d These provide plenty of opportunity for the *warehousing* of all kinds of cargoes.
e Bland had just finished a *report* on the subject I *mentioned*.
f Often single consignments are *divided* between two or more *boats*.

g These are *allotted* to each store according to individual *requirements*.

3 Answer these questions orally:

a Why is Hong Kong an ideal storehouse for transit goods to and from Asia?
b How are cargoes handled in Hong Kong harbour?
c What problems are caused by the clutter of lighters in the harbour?
d What did Mr Bland have to say about consolidation?

4 Question for discussion. What is the best port in your country? Why? How are cargoes handled there?

5 Write an essay of 400–600 words on any port that you know of, describing its advantages and disadvantages.

18 Manufacturer, Wholesaler, Retailer

Announcer: This is B.B.C., Radio Four, and here is Mary Owen to introduce the fourth programme in our series 'The Business World'.

Owen: Good evening. Our guest speakers tonight are Mr Charles Brand, representing the manufacturer, Mr Daniel Rhodes, from the wholesale business, and Mr Frank Berry, a retailer. Mr Brand, do you think the manufacturer would be better off without the middleman?

Brand: Well, Miss Owen, this is something every manufacturer has to think of at some time, but I think he generally finds in the final analysis he saves himself a whole lot of expense and trouble by getting someone else to look after his distribution problems. There are some exceptions of course, like manufacturers of heavy machinery and office equipment for example.

Owen: Will he really save himself expense?

Brand: Not always – in the case of a big manufacturer operating a mail order business for instance he may save by having his own mailing department. But in the case of goods sold in shops, most firms have found it pays to get someone else to do the retailing.

Owen: You haven't said anything about the wholesaler. Let's ask our retailer, Mr Berry, whether he thinks the wholesaler could be done away with.

Berry: From my personal point of view, the big advantage is the wholesaler can keep much bigger stocks than I'd want to have on my hands.

Rhodes: Perhaps I could add a word to defend my position as a wholesaler. One big service we do give is in helping both manufacturer and retailer with our store of information – knowledge of the trade, experience in forecasting market trends, changes in fashion and taste – things like that.

Owen: I suppose the wholesaler's also useful to the retailer in finding sources of supply?

	Rhodes:	Yes, and to the manufacturer in finding new outlets for his products.
	Berry:	Then we mustn't forget that wholesalers sometimes help the retailer with special credit terms.
	Brand:	I don't think we've mentioned that the wholesaler also bears a considerable risk when market prices change.
	Owen:	But he may stand to gain by this.
	Rhodes:	No-one takes a risk unless they think there's a chance of winning, do they?
	Brand:	That's a thought. – Another thing we haven't brought up is that the wholesalers often look after the cost and problems of publicity campaigns.
	Rhodes:	That's true. But what's even more important is that, by the orders he places with the manufacturer, the wholesaler largely guides production, because the manufacturer's likely to base his production planning at least to some extent on the wholesale orders he's getting.
	Berry:	I'd like to mention that most manufacturers wouldn't want the kind of small orders we smaller retailers put in. It's the wholesaler that takes the big order from the manufacturer, breaks bulk and lets each retailer have his small share of the order.
	Owen:	So far we've mostly heard the advantages of dealing with a wholesaler. How about some of the reasons for eliminating him?
	Brand:	Manufacturers of some proprietary articles prefer to deal direct with the retailer because they feel they get better publicity that way.
	Berry:	If the retailer's willing and able to buy large quantities, he may be better off buying direct from the factory.
	Owen:	Well, on the whole it looks as if the present set-up is likely to continue for some time at least. Thank you gentlemen, and goodnight – everybody.
	Announcer:	You have been listening to . . . .

NOTES

6 **wholesale**: sale of commodities to retailers rather than direct to consumers.

7 **retailer**: one who sells commodities to ultimate consumers, usually in small quantities.

8 **better off**: in a better position.
9 **middleman**: intermediary who distributes goods from producer to consumer on his own account and risk.
12 **in the final analysis**: in the end.
19 **a mail order business**: firm which receives orders and cash from buyers and sends goods to them.
25 **done away with**: eliminated, removed, got rid of.
37 **outlets**: ways of selling, places to sell through.
40 **credit terms**: arrangements for paying for goods later or by instalments.
43 **stand to**: be in a position to.
46 **that's a thought**: that's worth considering.
63 **proprietary**: manufactured and sold only by the owner of the patent, formula, brand name or trademark associated with the product.
68 **set-up**: arrangement.

Practice

1 Someone asks you what the above radio programme was about. Give them a summary of the programme in indirect speech, mentioning who said what.

2 In different countries, different articles are sold from different kinds of outlets. In England, for example, you can buy films at the chemists', in the USA you can buy almost anything at a drug-store. Nowadays, many car service stations are carrying an increasing range of articles.

a What outlets are used in your country for the following:

aspirin	nylon stockings	fishing-line
cigarettes	razor blades	postcards
matches	sweets	combs
electric batteries	tooth-brushes	flower-seeds
pens	shoe-polish	pins

b Using your knowledge of other countries as an aid, suggest further possible outlets for the above articles.

19 The European Market Place (1)

Social Change and Consumer's Choice

Before many years are out it will be commonplace for marketing men to look on the countries of Western Europe as one huge area of potential customers. The Common Market challenges them to plan their strategy on a scale to match the bounds of the Continent. What will this entail? Town life and home life, patterns of consumption and labour conditions, the structure of the distributive trades and the impact of mass media – we shall need to study all this and much else if we want to keep ahead of developments and take the right decisions to meet them. The executive's grasp of the future will depend on how sensitive he is to all that is going on around him. The question is: just how far do we understand the processes in which we find ourselves involved?

Take the rising standard of living. This is not one single, simple process. It may be true, as has been argued, that all European countries are travelling the same road towards what has been called 'salvation through industrialization', and it may be possible, therefore, to forecast some of the probable changes in living habits as the process continues. Even so, there are still great differences between one place and another, between one nation and another, and in the rates at which they change. These differences reveal themselves in a great diversity of what people want to buy. Economic development is certainly affecting culture and customs, habits and attitudes, traditions and mentality; but these, in turn, are reacting on what is going on in the economy – in production, consumption and distribution. You may detect the general trend; but look around Western Europe and you will discover all sorts of subtle variations in the speed and character of the change. Here the emancipation of women may be moving more slowly. There peasant and aristocratic attitudes may persist. The Netherlands and Sweden had their industrial revolutions late. In consequence, their cities, unlike some others elsewhere, do not have to struggle against the inheritance of the coal and steam age. In Belgium, by contrast, the antagonism between the Walloon and the Flemish parts has been largely explained by the differences between older and newer industrial settings. In the Flemish part the rise of the new, affluent middle classes took place under much more favourable conditions. All this colours domestic habits and the attitudes of people towards products.

Can we identify these subtle distinctions to a point where we can use our understanding of them to forecast social change? Market research, to be sure, does reveal social and cultural change. Consumer goods give evidence, in the jargon of business, of 'innovation-mindedness', 'achievement-orientedness' or 'cultural lags'. Some marketing companies collect an impressive bundle of facts about some characteristics of modern society. There is a growing volume of empirical findings about people's behaviour as consumers. To generalize from these facts, however, is not so easy. It requires a well-organized, systematic effort before the social scientist can contribute to long-term policy.

One question indicates the complexity of the problem. Why are people more ready to change their habitual behaviour in one direction than in another?

It seems to be easier, for instance for people to become familiar with refrigerators, washing-machines, vacuum cleaners, television sets and other technical novelties than it is for them to change their pattern of food habits or the style of their furniture and houses. Forecasts have been made of how many people will buy and own various household appliances in ten years' time, but who is going to forecast the qualitative changes in the delicate fields of food and domestic taste?

[ZAHN E. 'The European Market Place' – *Progress*, September 1962]

NOTES

2 **out**: gone by, past.

2 **commonplace**: usual.

4 **the Common Market**: the European Economic Community (EEC) consisting of France, Western Germany, Italy, Belgium, Holland and Luxembourg.

5 **bounds**: limits.

5 **the Continent**: Europe.

6 **entail**: mean.

17 **salvation**: being saved (in this case from poverty).

This is the age of the Auto-Jet!

Today's dishwasher — family-sized, efficient and low priced.
Let Hoover Auto-Jet open your eyes to what a dishwasher should be. Nothing half-hearted about the Auto-Jet! It's the complete, final, affordable answer to who does the washing-up . . . the drying-up . . . the whole age-old problem. Read the facts. Then see the Auto-Jet for yourself.

21 **rates**: speed.
24 **mentality**: way of thinking.
26 **detect**: find out, discover.
27 **subtle**: delicate, hard to distinguish.
28 **emancipation of**: giving of equal rights to.
33 **antagonism**: opposition.
36 **affluent**: wealthy, rich.
38 **colours**: affects, changes.
43 **innovation-mindedness**: interest in new things.
44 **achievement-orientedness**: desire to achieve certain goals.
44 **cultural lags**: being behind the general 'level of progress'.
47 **empirical**: from experience or observation.
52 **habitual**: usual, customary.
59 **household appliances**: machines used in the house, such as vacuum cleaners and refrigerators.

Practice

1 Give your own definitions of the meaning of the following as they are used in the above passage. Write your own definitions first, then look the words up to check their meaning.

potential	reveal	delicate
to challenge	diversity	qualitative
strategy	react	complexity
to match	variation	systematic
pattern	inheritance	volume
impact	by contrast	identify
mass media	setting	distinction
to forecast	novelty	in consequence

When you have checked your definitions, put the words and expressions in sentences of your own.

2a Make verbs from the following:

consumption	revelation	familiar
decision	production	argument
grasp	variation	revolution

Put your verbs in sentences of your own.

b Make adjectives from the following:

strategy	distribute	continue (2)
diversity	persist	antagonism
quality	system	habit

Put your adjectives in sentences of your own.

3 Answer the following orally:
a What must we study to keep ahead of developments in the European market place? Several things are mentioned in the passage; mention these and try to add to them.
b What examples does the author give of change (and lack of change) in economic development in Western Europe? What examples can you give with reference to your own country?

4 Write an essay of 400-600 words on changes in pattern or style in one or several of the following:

a food habits
b furniture
c housing
d household appliances

20 Consumer Guidance

The Consumers' Association (CA) has formed a panel to discuss the effect of consumer guidance on the public and on business life in Britain. The Chairman is a member of the staff of CA.

Chairman: Good evening, ladies and gentlemen. I'd like to begin by saying just a few words about CA. As we all know, the business of making and selling is highly organized, often in large units, and calls to its aid at every step complex and highly expert skills. The business of buying, on the other hand, is conducted by the smallest unit, the individual consumer, relying on the guidance afforded by experience, if he possesses it, and if not, on instinctive but not always rational thought processes. We of the Consumers' Association – which is an independent, non-profit-making organization – aim at redressing this imbalance between the power of the seller and the power of the buyer. We test products, investigate services, and publish frank comparative reports on their quality and value. – Well, that's enough about us. Now to introduce our panel members. On my right here is Mrs Sheila Thompson, a housewife. On my left, Mr Lionel Denton, a business man. And our first question is, do you think CA has had any real effect on the position of the consumer in this country? Mrs Thompson.

Thompson: Oh yes, I'm sure it has. I take your magazine *Which?* every month, and I can't imagine how I managed without it before. I'm positive we've saved hundreds of pounds taking your advice about the best fridge to buy, and the best cosmetics, and the best things to buy when you're on holiday in Europe – oh, and all sorts of things.

Chairman: Well, it's very nice to hear we've been of use to you, Mrs Thompson. What would you say about this, Mr Denton?

Denton: First, from the point of view of the average consumer,

	I think CA has done something to make him – or her – more aware of what's available. From my personal standpoint, I'm not a regular subscriber to *Which?*, but I did come across an excellent 'Borrowing Supplement' and a sound report on Mortgages.
Chairman:	What about the manufacturer's point of view?
Denton:	If a firm's making a product of inferior quality and charging an unreasonable price for it, it won't like the CA report, of course. But in my opinion a genuinely worthwhile product need fear nothing, and the maker should be glad of the publicity he gets through *Which?*. And another thing, he should be able to learn something about what the public wants by seeing the relative value given in reports to different qualities of a product.
Chairman:	Thank you. Our next question is, how extensive should the activities of CA be?
Thompson:	I'd say just as widespread as possible. For instance, it's a wonderful thing if an independent body gives publicity to how long people have to queue for hospital appointments. After all, it's the tax-payers who have to pay for our hospital service, so why shouldn't they see it's run properly?
Denton:	I'd like to put in a word for the reports on various kinds of insurance. It's that kind of really big unit the consumer has to keep an eye on. How about a CA report on the various members of the Government, showing whether they're pulling their weight or not?
Chairman:	Now you're really giving us a big job to do. Well, the next question for discussion is . . . .

NOTES

11 **instinctive**: following an inborn pattern of response.
12 **rational**: logical.
14 **redressing**: putting right.
15 **imbalance**: lack of balance.
17 **frank**: honest, sincere, outspoken.
28 **fridge**: (colloquial) short for refrigerator.
38 **standpoint**: point of view.

38 **subscriber**: one who buys regularly.
39 **supplement**: additional feature of a magazine or newspaper.
40 **mortgages**: money raised against the security of property (especially houses or land).
63 **pulling their weight**: doing their job properly.

Practice

1 A panel discussion. Students are chosen to be on a panel of 3 to 4 persons, one of whom is appointed Chairman. The general subject for discussion is 'Consumer Guidance in Our Country', and the panel is required to answer such questions as:
a What form does consumer guidance take (if any)?
b Would more consumer guidance be a good thing? In what form?
c Is advertising a satisfactory form of consumer guidance?
d What products or services would the panel like to have consumer guidance on? Why?
e What do you think of the work of the Consumer Association in Britain? How does it compare with similar bodies in your country?
f What do you think would be the attitude of the business world to consumer guidance?
Students can be asked to supply further questions. The teacher can decide whether or not the panel are given an opportunity to prepare their answers.

2 Do-it-yourself consumer guidance. Choose one of the following or take some product or service of your own choice.

cameras, refrigerators, life insurance, electric irons, lipsticks, drip-dry shirts, sunglasses, TV sets, portable typewriters, cars within a certain range.

When you have made your choice, list the comparative qualities of the different makes of products or services offered on the market in your country. (As this will mean quite a lot of research work, it may be best for the class to work in teams). Suggested qualities for comparison (these will vary according to the article in question):

price, durability, advantages offered, safety, size, quietness, efficiency, ease of use, service available, running costs, resale price, etc.

Finally give a rating to each product or service. Ratings:
- *a* Best buy
- *b* Good value for money
- *c* Reasonable
- *d* Below standard

21 The European Market Place (2)

Consumer Behaviour and Decisions

Delicate factors behind demand – demand for prestige, for recognition and for reassurance about one's role and place in society – have acted as an immense stimulus to the psychological refinement of products. Market research is leaving behind its original character of pure commercial fact-finding. In advertising, there is a shift of emphasis from the technical characteristics of the product to the social and psychological meanings. There is supply and demand on the subtle and sensitive level of symbols and images.

The approach of the Common Market emphasizes the importance of this. For product images vary from country to country. The same product may be a prestige item in one area and quite common in another. In England, beer is a common thing but wine is a luxury; in Portugal it is sometimes the other way round.

Some products are more cosmopolitan in their appeal than others. In the Netherlands, cigarettes can only be sold in English packages which give the illusion that they come from England or the United States. The word cigarette is never printed in the Dutch spelling. Tests have revealed that some people associate the look of the Dutch word *sigaret* unconsciously with the lower class, or 'the poor'. The contrary is true in the case of cigars. These are upper-class symbols, appealing to the Dutch national consciousness and bearing names of Dutch history. In France, the cigarette has a French image (Gauloises, Gitanes); this image is so typical that its prestige value is felt in Switzerland and Belgium, where one can buy cigarettes with the French appeal.

Britain has a comparatively low replacement rate for domestic furniture and cars. We are told that the 'middle-class conservatism of suburbia is still solidly in favour of reproduction furniture', and *The Times Review of British Industry* has called car designs 'conventional and to some extent unimaginative'. Some new markets in household appliances seem to confirm rather than contradict the general picture of conservatism. The success of electric blankets is said to be due to the lack of central heating.

Consumer Investment

Consumer durables or consumer investment items are a matter of 'outlays of choice' rather than of routine buying. In 'higher income group' countries such as Switzerland, where people spend about twenty-eight per cent of their money on food (including a wide choice of luxury items), there is plenty left for outlays of choice or 'discretionary spending' on other goods and services, but in such countries as Greece (fifty-eight per cent of income spent on food) the customer's influence is proportionately lessened. In other words, in an affluent society consumers have more chance to influence the economy through their decisions.

The attention of consumer research is, therefore, particularly focused on decision making. What factors contribute to specific buying decisions in the household, and what do we know about the processes of decision making? Rising young families are more likely to be 'innovation leaders'; they have visions of a rising standard of living and problems posed by the need to care for young children. Where a major improvement is needed in the housework's productivity because of the demands made upon the housewife, investment in labour-saving equipment is more likely. Households are expanding firms, and family growth is, just like a growing business corporation, a challenge to long-term planning.

Consumer goods are the contemporary type of personal property. That has been the case since the ancient types of property such as land, factories and other sorts of production goods were transferred from the well-to-do families to corporations or the state. Market research people are studying the roles and meanings of goods within the contemporary patterns of family careers and suburban life.

Thus what we call 'consumer behaviour' is much more than an economic occurrence. It stands for contemporary attitudes and expectations, for aspirations and ambitions. People are not mechanical users of goods and services but choosers of ways of living in a changing world. That has its consequences for business and implies new responsibilities.

[ZAHN, E. 'The European Market Place'. *Progress*, September 1962]

NOTES

10 **approach**: way of looking at, handling something.
15 **appeal**: attraction, interest they offer.
27 **replacement rate**: rate at which new articles are bought to replace old ones of the same kind.
29 **suburbia**: residential suburbs of big cities, especially London.
29 **reproduction furniture**: furniture the style of which is copied from some well-known original.
37 **outlays**: expenditure.
41 **discretionary**: according to one's choice, not because of necessity.
47 **focused on**: directed towards.
51 **posed by**: arising from, due to.
57 **contemporary**: of our time.
66 **aspirations**: what one wishes for, would like to have or be.
68 **implies**: means, suggests.

Practice

1 Give your own definitions of the meaning of the following as they are used in the above passage. Write your own definitions first, then look up the words to check their meaning.

prestige	luxury	corporation
reassurance	cosmopolitan	to transfer
role	illusion	consumer durable
stimulus	to associate	occurrence
refinement	contrary	ambition
market research	to appeal	specific
shift	routine	innovation
subtle	services	productivity
symbol	affluent	consequence
image	investment	suburban

When you have checked your definitions, put the words and expressions in sentences of your own.

2a What countries do the following come from:

the Dutch, the Flemish, the Swiss, the Portuguese, the Welsh, the Turks, the Danes, the Greeks.

b What people live in:

Europe, China, the U.K., Japan, the U.S.S.R., Norway, Poland, Peru, Egypt.

3 Questions for discussion:

a What products are normally sold under a foreign name in your country? What languages are most popular? What products are sold under the native language?
b Mention some examples of outlays of choice that you have made recently.
c Do you consider your society an affluent one? Why (not)?
d Say why you think people buy the following:

vacuum cleaners, art paintings, new houses, land, sports cars, fur coats, wine, Scandinavian furniture, sailing boats, foreign foodstuffs.

5 Write an essay of from 400–600 words on 'Consumer Behaviour in My Country'.

22 Consumer Motivation

The canned foods firm for which David Simpson works has invited a visiting speaker to lead a discussion on 'Consumer Motivation and Eating Habits'. Simpson has been given the task of chairing the meeting.

Simpson: Ladies and gentlemen, it gives me great pleasure to introduce our guest speaker tonight. As we all know, Sir Claud is one of Britain's leading lights in the realm of consumer research, and we certainly appreciate his kindness in giving up his valuable time to us this evening. Ladies and gentlemen, Sir Claud O'Connell.

O'Connell: Thank you, Mr Chairman, and good evening to you, ladies and gentlemen. Well, you'll no doubt be relieved to hear that I'm not going to deliver a long and erudite speech on the mysteries of my subject. I'm just going to start off what I hope will be a lively and fruitful discussion by saying a few introductory words.

Consumer motivation, which is just a fancy name for what makes people adopt certain buying habits, is one of those things we all talk about nowadays, but none of us knows much about. We talk about fashions – what are fashions? We divide people up into different classes of consumers – Early Adopters, Late Adopters and what have you. We invent terms like 'outlays of choice'. But we can only guess why, for example, the French eat ten times as much soup as the English, and the Scots four times as much. What part do social conventions play, how powerful is the role of advertising? What influence does the climate have on food purchases? If you asked the man in the street why the Italians drink far less milk than the Swiss, I'm willing to bet he'd say it must have something to do with the climate – or the cows. But what about the fact that eighty-five per cent of all Italian infants are nursed by their mothers during the first three months of their lives, compared with only forty-five per cent in Switzerland? The point I'm trying to make is, nothing is self-evident in this field.

Well, that's enough from me – let's see if we can together formulate some provisional answers to questions like those I've thrown out. How about starting off with the effect of the rise in the standard of living?

Simpson: Thank you, Sir Claud. Now ladies and gentlemen, your comments please.

Bellamy: Well – er – since nobody else seems willing to start the ball rolling, I'd just like to make a small comment. I have an idea – may easily be complete nonsense of course – that though a higher standard of living makes people buy more expensive things, it won't necessarily change their tastes and preferences.

O'Connell: No, I quite agree with you there. Take these Italian restaurants that have sprung up all over London in the past few years. They haven't changed the pattern of English eating, they've just added to it. In fact, it's a question of evolution, not revolution.

Mrs Bedford: Mr Chairman, I'd like to ask a question if I may. Sir Claud, my impression is that in spite of all these new easy-to-prepare foods, cooking isn't going out by any means. Why is this?

O'Connell: My personal opinion is that much of the drudgery has been taken out of cooking, so that people can concentrate on the 'culinary art' as it's called and really treat it as an art.

Mrs Bedford: D'you think people are becoming more imaginative cooks then, even in England?

O'Connell: Oh yes, especially among the better-educated classes. Cooking's become a smart hobby you see. And of course the mechanized kitchen and the stylish design of household machinery have helped – they've even tempted quite a few husbands into the kitchen I understand.

Simpson: Would anyone else like to comment? Yes – there at the back – Mr Lessing, isn't it?

(*The discussion continues*)

NOTES

4 **chairing**: acting as chairman.
7 **leading lights**: most prominent persons.
8 **realm**: field.
14 **relieved**: pleased because something unpleasant, boring, etc. is not going to happen.
15 **erudite**: learned.
17 **fruitful**: profitable, useful.
19 **fancy**: high-sounding.
25 **and what have you**: and so on.
29 **conventions**: accepted usage.
36 **nursed**: given milk.
39 **self-evident**: completely clear.
41 **formulate**: express in precise form.
41 **provisional**: temporary, for the time being, not final.
42 **thrown out**: suggested at random.
47 **start the ball rolling**: begin the discussion.
49 **have an idea**: think.
54 **sprung up**: spring-sprang-sprung: appeared.
57 **evolution**: natural development.
57 **revolution**: sudden, complete change.
60 **going out**: disappearing, becoming unfashionable.
62 **drudgery**: dull work.
69 **smart**: fashionable.
72 **tempted**: persuaded, attracted.

Practice

1 Listen to the recording of this dialogue or get students to read it aloud. The rest of the class keeps minutes of the meeting (see Chapter 12, Practice 1.).

2 Prepare short speeches lasting about three minutes. Suggested subjects:

a Cooking in my country
b Psychological factors behind demand
c Prestige articles
d Consolidation

e Containerization
f Types of packaging material
g Dual-purpose packaging
h Developments in road transport
i Problems of the executive
j Labour problems

While the speeches are being made, the rest of the class can take notes on them and write short reports from their notes.

Glossary of Commercial Terms used in the Book

Explanations are given in a limited vocabulary of 4,000 words. Pronunciation is given in the simplified IPA transcription used in such publications as *English Language Teaching*.

abstain [əb'stein]: not do something; *abstain from voting* = not vote either for or against.

access ['akses]: the way into a place; *easy of access* = easily reached, easy to enter.

accommodate [ə'komədeit]: have room for; *accommodation* [əˌkomə'deiʃn] = a place to live in or sleep in; an *accommodation allowance* is a fixed amount of money to pay for such a place, e.g. a hotel room.

accountant [ə'kauntənt]: a person who keeps or checks business accounts.

achievement-orientedness [ə'tʃiːvmənt,oːrientidnis]: a desire to achieve or reach certain goals.

acquisition [ˌakwi'ziʃn]: acquiring, getting control of by buying etc.

adaptable [ə'daptəbl]: easily made suitable for different purposes.

adjourn [ə'dʒəːn]: end (a meeting) for the present, with the intention of meeting again later.

adjust [ə'dʒʌst]: change (something) to suit particular circumstances; *adjustment* [ə'dʒʌstmənt] making changes to meet a situation.

adopt [ə'dopt]: accept; pass or carry a motion, a majority having voted in favour of it; *early adopters* [ə'doptəz] are quick to follow a new fashion, buy new inventions etc.

advisory [əd'vaizəri]: giving advice; *in an advisory capacity* = as an adviser.

aerosol ['eərousol]: a container from which a liquid under pressure can be released in a spray.

affluent ['afluənt]: wealthy.

agenda [ə'dʒendə]: list of matters to be dealt with and discussed, in the order in which the conference or meeting will deal with them.

air space ['eə ˌspeis]: space required for one's goods on one or more aircraft.

airfreight ['eəfreit]: transporting goods by air.

allocate ['aloukeit]: share out (duties etc.); *re-allocate* ['riː'aloukeit] = distribute in a new way.

analysis [ə'nalisis]: *in the final analysis* = in the end, when everything has been considered.

appendix [ə'pendiks]: extra material at the end of a book or of a set of papers (plural: *appendices* [ə'pendisiːz] or (esp. of books) *appendixes* [ə'pendiksiz]).

appliance [ə'plaiəns]: a piece of machinery; *household appliances* = machines used in the house, such as vacuum cleaners and refrigerators.

approximate [ə'proksimit]: perhaps not exact but very nearly right.

aptitude [ˈaptitjuːd]: fitness, probable ability to do a job or to learn.

area [ˈeəriə]: place considered as a surface. The word is used rather loosely for a particular part of a more general problem or situation, e.g. *areas of mutual interest* = things that we all want and can therefore agree on.

assess [əˈses]: decide on the value, importance etc. of something.

assignment [əˈsainmənt]: piece of work that an employee is ordered to do.

B/L – see *bill of lading*

background [ˈbakgraund]: a person's education, experience etc.

belonging [biˈloŋiŋ]: being a member; a *sense of belonging* = a feeling that you are one of a team.

bill of lading [ˈbil əv ˈleidiŋ]: a receipt for goods loaded on a ship.

board meeting [ˈboːd ˌmiːtiŋ]: meeting of the directors to decide the policy of a firm.

boom [buːm]: (have) a great increase in trade and wealth.

break bulk – see *bulk*.

brink [briŋk]: edge, with danger lying beyond it.

broker [ˈbroukə]: a man whose profession is that of a middleman in some special field such as buying and selling stocks and shares (a *stockbroker* [ˈstokbroukə]), arranging for the hire or charter of ships (a *ship-broker* [ˈʃipbroukə]) etc.

bulk [bʌlk]: large quantity; *break bulk* = divide up large items into smaller parts, e.g. removing the contents of a standard container.

CA [ˈsiːˈei] – see *Consumer's Association*

canteen [kanˈtiːn]: a firm's own restaurant.

car ferry – see *ferry*.

chair [tʃeə]: *the Chair* = the *chairman* [ˈtʃeəmən]. At a formal meeting you *address the Chair*.

chartering [ˈtʃaːtəriŋ]: hiring (a ship).

climatic [klaiˈmatik]: of climate (general weather conditions).

code [koud]: a system of signs or numbers to save space or words; *code number* = a number which represents something, e.g. a price, a name and address, a telephone exchange etc.

Common Market – see *European Economic Community*.

communicate [kəˈmjuːnikeit]: make oneself understood.

competent [ˈkompitənt]: able to do (something) well, e.g. a *competent performer* has the ability, skill or knowledge to do a job properly.

complex [ˈkompleks]: made up of several different parts and therefore difficult; the opposite of simple; n. *complexity* [komˈpleksiti].

comprehensive [ˌkompriˈhensiv]: covering everything, e.g. a *comprehensive service* given by a firm of packers will include collection, packing and forwarding.

computer [kemˈpjuːtə]: electronic calculating machine; the *computer age* is a name for the present time, when decisions based on the calculations of computers influence our lives more every day.

concentrate [ˈkɔnsəntreit]: bring together in one place; *concentrate on* = give all one's attention to.

concept [ˈkɔnsept]: idea.

concession [kənˈseʃn]: something that is allowed or granted, e.g. *tax concessions* mean reduced taxes to encourage exporters etc.

confirm [kənˈfɔːm]: say or prove that something is right.

conservatism [kənˈsəːvətizm]: unwillingness to change.

consign [kənˈsain]: send; *consignment* [kənˈsainmənt] = goods sent at one time to one person or firm; *consignee* [ˌkɔnsaiˈniː] = the person to whom a consignment is sent.

consolidate [kənˈsɔlideit]: bring together in one large unit; n. *consolidation* [kənˌsɔliˈdeiʃn].

consume [kənˈsjuːm]: use up; *time consumer* [ˈtaim kənˌsjuːmə] = something that uses up a lot of time.

Consumers' Association: an organization to guide consumers, as explained in Chapter 20.

consumption [kənˈsʌmpʃn]: the use; the amount used.

containerization [kənˌteinəraiˈzeiʃn]: the use of standard containers as explained in Chapter 13.

contemporary [kənˈtempərəri]: of today, of modern times.

continent [ˈkɔntinənt]: one of the world's great land masses; *the Continent* = Europe, especially Western Europe not including the British Isles.

contribution [ˌkɔntriˈbjuːʃn]: something which is given; the *contribution* of a meeting is the amount of help it gives towards reaching policy decisions etc.

cope [koup]: be successful in managing or handling; *cope with* = deal successfully with.

course [kɔːs]: direction to follow; a *course of action* = things that must be done.

crane [krein]: a machine for lifting heavy loads, e.g. on or off a ship.

culture [ˈkʌltʃə]: (sometimes) a stage of social advance; *cultural lag* [ˈkʌltʃərəl ˈlag] = being behind the general level of progress.

definition [ˌdefiˈniʃn]: clear statement (of meaning).

delivery [diˈlivəri]: causing (something) to arrive; the *due delivery date* = the day by which the customer has been promised that the goods will arrive.

denote [diˈnout]: show, stand for, be a sign for (e.g. *Red denotes the London area*).

destination [ˌdestiˈneiʃn]: place to which a person or thing is going.

dictate [dikˈteit]: say the words that are to be typed in a letter etc. Sometimes a secretary takes down this *dictation* [dikˈteiʃn] in *shorthand* (see below), and sometimes the words are spoken to a recording machine such as a *dictaphone* [ˈdiktəfoun].

dimension [diˈmenʃn]: measurement, e.g. length, breadth, height etc.

discount [ˈdiskaunt]: a reduction of price for certain reasons.

discretion [disˈkreʃn]: choice; *discretionary* [disˈkreʃənəri] *spending* = paying for goods and services that are not the ordinary necessities of life.

dispatch [dis'patʃ]: send(ing) out; the *dispatch bay* is the part of a factory from which goods are sent.

disposable [dis'pouzəbl]: (easily) destroyed or got rid of.

disposal [dis'pouzl]: *at your disposal* = which you are able to use.

docker ['dokə]: dock worker; man whose work is loading and unloading ships.

document ['dokjumənt]: official papers; *documentation* [,dokjumen'teiʃn] the various documents needed for a particular purpose, e.g. for exporting goods by ship.

downward ['daunwəd]: becoming less or worse.

dual-purpose ['djuəl'pə:pəs]: having two uses.

durability [,dju:rə'biliti]: the quality of being *durable* (see Book 1 Glossary) or made to last a long time.

EEC ['i:,i:'si:] – see *European Economic Community*.

eliminate [i'limineit]: make (someone or something) unnecessary and get rid of (him or it) for that reason.

encase [in'keis]: put into a box or other container.

enlarge [in'la:dʒ]: make bigger; to *enlarge on* an idea is to say more about it.

entrepôt ['ontrəpou]: port or commercial centre which handles goods imported for re-export.

European Economic Community (also called the *Common Market* or *EEC*) the association of France, Western Germany, Italy, Belgium, Holland and Luxemburg.

eventual [i'ventʃuəl]: final, e.g. the *eventual destination* of goods arriving at Hong Kong may be somewhere in Japan.

expertise [,ekspə:'ti:z]: expert knowledge, knowing the best way to do something and being able to do it particularly well.

external [eks'tə:nl]: on the outside; *external presentation* – see *presentation*.

extrusion [eks'tru:ʒn]: something that is made by pressing a melted metal or plastic through a narrow opening of a particular shape.

feather-bedding ['feðəbediŋ]: avoiding work, often by keeping more workers than are needed.

ferry ['feri]: a boat or ship that carries people or goods from one side to the other of a (fairly narrow) piece of water; a *car ferry* ['ka:,feri] is a ship specially designed to carry cars.

flexible ['fleksəbl]: easily changed; able to do things in more than one way; (of materials) easy to bend.

fluent [fluənt]: speaking easily and without hesitation.

foothold ['futhould]: an established position from which to make further progress.

forecast ['fo:ka:st]: say what the future will probably bring.

foresight ['fo:sait]: ability to see into the future or to imagine what the future may bring.

formulate ['fo:mjuleit]: express clearly and exactly.

freeport ['fri:po:t]: (of a port) where there are no customs charges or duties.

freight [freit]: the transport of goods; the cost of such transport.

friction ['frikʃn]: causes of unfriendliness and quarrels.

fringe [frindʒ]: an edge or outer part; *fringe benefits* ['frindʒ ˌbenifits] = advantages besides pay and working conditions for the employees of a firm, e.g. free medical care.

functional ['fʌŋkʃənl]: connected with the way a thing works or the purpose for which it was made.

geographical [dʒiə'grafikl]: concerned with position on the surface of the Earth.

guidance ['gaidəns]: advice; *consumer guidance* = advice given to consumers, those who buy goods for their own use.

hardware ['haːdweə]: metal goods such as tools, knives, locks etc.

haulage ['hoːlidʒ]: transport of goods; *road haulage* = carrying goods by road in lorries etc; *haulers* ['hoːləz] or *hauliers* ['hoːljəz] = a firm that does this work.

home [houm]: one's own country; the *home market* is the opposite of the export market.

house magazine ['haus ˌmagə'ziːn]: a weekly or monthly paper for members of the firm.

impulse-buying ['impʌlsˌbaiiŋ]: buying something when you see it, not as a result of a previous plan or intention.

incentive [in'sentiv]: something that encourages people to work harder.

industrial revolution [in'dʌstriəl ˌrevə'luːʃn]: (historically) the great changes that came with the introduction of power-driven machinery into the methods of production.

inferior [in'fiəriə]: not so good, not good enough.

initiative [i'niʃiətiv]: ability to see what should be done and to do it.

innovation [ˌinou'veiʃn]: introducing new ideas and making changes; *innovation leaders* = those people who will be the first to buy new things; *innovation-mindedness* = an interest in new things; an *innovator* ['inouveitə] is not afraid to make changes.

insight ['insait]: ability to see into and understand something; *psychological* [ˌsaikə'lodʒikl] *insight* = ability to see how other people's minds work.

install [in'stoːl]: put into position.

integrated ['intigreitid]: made up into a single whole.

interpret [in'təːprit]: give immediately in one language the meaning of words spoken in another language. There is always work for a good *interpreter* [in'təːpritə] who can do this well.

key [kiː]: essential, important, central, vital; if you find the answer to a *key question*, you will have no difficulty with related questions; the success of a firm depends on the work of a few executives in *key positions*.

knowledge worker ['nolidʒ ˌwəːkə]: person who is employed for his scientific or other special knowledge.

labour relations ['leibə riˌleiʃnz]: the attitude of workers to management and of executives to other employees.

lading – see *bill of lading*.

lay-off ['leiof]: telling employees that there is no work for them. A *lay-off* is usually temporary (i.e. for a limited time) and not permanent like dismissal or redundancy.

long-range ['loŋ'reindʒ]: for the more distant future.

long-term ['loŋ'tə:m]: intended to last a long time.

mail order ['meil ,o:də]: a *mail order business* = a firm which receives orders and cash from members of the public and sends goods in return, usually by post.

manual ['manjuəl]: using the hands; a *manual worker* works with his hands, using tools, machines etc, unlike clerical workers (in the office), draftsmen (in the drawing office) etc.

market patterns ['ma:kit ,patənz] – see *pattern*.

marshal ['ma:ʃl]: bring together and arrange; a *marshalling point* = place where goods are brought together, e.g. for making up container loads.

mass media ['mas 'mi:diə]: the ways of getting information to great numbers of the public – radio, TV, newspapers etc.

memorandum [,memə'randəm]: a report.

middleman ['midlman]: wholesaler (see Book 1); *broker* (see above); person involved in trade but not the producer or the final seller.

mimeograph ['mimiəgra:f]: (make copies with) a machine for making large numbers of copies of typed material.

minimize ['minimaiz]: make as small as possible.

minutes ['minits]: official record of what is said and decided at a meeting; a secretary *keeps the minutes* = makes notes at a meeting and develops the notes into formal minutes.

mobility [mou'biliti]: ability to move or to be moved; *mobility of labour* = the willingness of workers to move from one place or job to another.

moor [muə]: tie up a ship; *mooring space* = place where ships can anchor or be tied up while in harbour.

mortgage ['mo:gidʒ]: money borrowed against the security of property (especially houses or land).

motion ['mouʃn]: proposal or formal statement to which a speaker wants a meeting to agree.

motivation [,mouti'veiʃn]: the reason why people act in a certain way; supplying a motive or reason for action; *consumer motivation* = the reasons behind people's buying habits or behind changes in demand for goods.

national consciousness ['naʃənl 'konʃəsnis]: being proud of one's country.

negotiations [ni,gouʃi'eiʃnz]: discussions in an attempt to reach agreement.

nomination [,nomi'neiʃn]: proposing someone as a candidate.

non-returnable ['nonri'tə:nəbl]: not to be returned, e.g. *non-returnable bottles* are not sent back to the maker of the contents to be used again.

objective [əb'dʒektiv]: seeing things from outside without being involved in one's own feelings.

off-loading ['of'loudiŋ]: unloading, especially from a ship.

order [ˈoːdə]: a *point of order* is a matter of correct *procedure* (see below) at a formal meeting.

outlay [ˈautlei]: money spent; *outlays of choice* = money spent on goods and services other than food and ordinary necessities.

overall [ˈouvərɔːl]: total; *overall consumption* = the total amount used.

overrule [ˌouvəˈruːl]: not allow (an objection), i.e. not agree that there is good cause.

overseas [ˈouvəsiːz]: in other countries.

overtime [ˈouvətaim]: working outside one's ordinary working hours; payment for such extra work.

panel [ˈpanl]: a group of speakers invited to discuss a subject or subjects in front of an audience.

paperboard [ˈpeipɔbɔːd]: card made from paper.

pattern [ˈpatən]: the way in which things are arranged; *market patterns* = what people want to buy in different places or at different times.

payload [ˈpeiloud]: the part of a load that is paid for (it includes the container).

personnel [ˌpəːsəˈnel]: the employees of a firm; a firm's *personnel department* deals with matters concerning the people who are employed by the firm; the head of this department is the *Personnel Manager*.

perspective [pəˈspektiv]: the right way of seeing things; *put things in perspective* = see things in proportion, or make others see all sides of a question.

plus value [ˈplʌs ˌvaljuː]: an advantage; something on the credit side.

PR [ˈpiːˈaː] – see *public relations*.

precise [priˈsais]: exact; a *precise figure* = an exact amount of money required as a fee or other payment.

presentation [ˌprezenˈteiʃn]: (1) introducing or explaining some matter; (2) (of a person) being of pleasant appearance, good manners etc; (3) being shown in an attractive form and package, as *external presentation*.

primary [ˈpraimɔri]: first; *primary products* = things produced by the land, sea etc, not by manufacture.

priority [praiˈoriti]: first importance; to *give* something *priority* is to treat it as more important than other matters.

procedure [prəˈsiːdʒə]: the correct way to do things.

product [ˈprodʌkt]: *product research* = research into ways of improving the thing produced (as distinct from market research to find out what people will buy).

production goods [prəˈdʌkʃn ˌgudz]: things that can be bought and sold but which themselves produce other goods, e.g. machines and factories.

project [ˈprodʒekt]: (as Book 1 Glossary and) a single piece of work for one or more firms, e.g. building a major bridge is a *project* which includes planning, drawing, steelwork, roadworks and many other branches of engineering.

promote [prəˈmout]: encourage; give a good start to (something).

proprietary [prəˈpraiətəri]: manufactured only by the owner of the patent etc.

provisional [prə'viʒənl]: for the present time, to be changed wholly or in part as circumstances require.

psychological [,saikə'lodʒikl]: based on the study of human behaviour and thought processes; the *psychological refinement* of a product = the ways in which it is made or presented in order to attract purchasers.

public relations ['pʌblik ri'leiʃnz]: giving out information about a company, government etc in order to gain the good opinion of the public; also called *PR*.

publicize ['pʌblisaiz]: give *publicity* (see Book 1 Glossary) to.

qualitative ['kwolitətiv]: in quality, usually as distinct from *quantitative* ['kwontitətiv] = in quantity or amount.

questionnaire [,kwestiə'neə]: a list of questions to be answered by every member of a group.

rational ['raʃənl]: by reasoning.

recommendation [,rekəmen'deiʃn]: advice; actions advised by somebody.

regulations [,regju'leiʃnz]: official rules and orders, e.g. a country's *trading regulations* are its laws, rules etc about trade.

repeat orders [ri'pi:t 'o:dəz]: more orders of the same kind.

replacement [ri'pleismənt]: buying a new article to take the place of an old one; *replacement rate* = how frequently people buy a new article, e.g. a new car.

requisite ['rekwizit]: required by the rules.

resale price ['ri:'seil ,prais]: the price the manufacturer expects the shop to charge.

restrictive [ri'striktiv]: limiting, not allowing freedom; *restrictive practices* in industry are actions that prevent competition or prevent the most efficient use of labour etc.

re-training ['ri:'treiniŋ]: teaching workers new trades, or new skills for their present jobs.

return [ri'tə:n]: profit, considered as a way of getting back a capital outlay.

rostrum ['rostrəm]: a platform for public speaking.

routine [ru:'ti:n]: things done in the usual way; *routine correspondence* = dealing with and writing letters on matters which need no special decisions.

running costs ['rʌniŋ ,kosts]: the money needed regularly for fuel or electricity, maintenance, etc, to use an article.

sack [sak]: dismiss from employment.

scrambler ['skramblə]: a machine which mixes the sounds a speaker makes (e.g. on the telephone) so that nobody can understand them until they are *unscrambled* by another machine.

second ['sekənd]: support a motion. A motion must be proposed by two speakers: the first *proposes* it, and the second *seconds* it ('I second the motion'), before it is debated.

session ['seʃn]: time between the beginning and end of a meeting; a conference is *in session* while it is assembled.

ship-broker – see *broker*.

shipment ['ʃipmənt]: putting on a ship; sending goods away (especially by ship).

shipping space ['ʃipiŋ ˌspeis]: space required for one's goods on a ship or ships.

shorthand ['ʃo:thand]: a system of special signs used for very rapid writing.

signify ['signifai]: make known; show how you wish to vote.

slinging ['sliŋiŋ]: *slinging positions* are the points to which ropes or chains are fastened for lifting and moving a container.

small-ads ['smo:ladz]: the small advertisements printed in columns according to the subject (e.g. 'Secretaries Wanted', 'Cars for Sale') in the newspapers.

socialize ['souʃəlaiz]: bring under State ownership and control.

specialist ['speʃəlist]: expert in one particular form of work; *specialist packers* = a firm which has developed particular skills and knowledge in packing goods for other firms.

spell out ['spel 'aut]: explain clearly, exactly and fully.

standardize ['standədaiz]: make (something) according to fixed standards.

stimulus ['stimjuləs]: a cause of activity.

strike [straik]: an organized refusal to work, officially called a 'withdrawal of labour'. We say that workers *strike* or *go on strike*; after that, they are *on strike*.

structural ['strʌktʃərl]: in the way it is built or made; the *structural strength* of a container is the way it is built to prevent damage to itself or its contents.

subordinate [sə'bo:dinit]: in a lower position or rank; an executive's *subordinates* are all those who receive their orders directly or indirectly from him.

subsistence [səb'sistəns]: food and drink; a *subsistence allowance* = money to pay for meals etc during time spent away from home.

suburb ['sʌbə:b]: one of the outer parts of a big city containing the houses of people who work in the city; *suburbia* [sə'bə:biə] refers collectively, and usually with some scorn, to the people who live in suburbs.

summary ['sʌməri]: short statement of the main points.

surplus ['sə:pləs]: amount left when all needs have been supplied; *surplus labour* = more men than jobs.

sustain [səs'tein]: support (an objection), i.e. agree that there is cause (for the objection).

symbol ['simbl]: visible sign of something, e.g. a *status symbol* ['steitəs 'simbl] = sign of importance, such as a fine office carpet or an efficient and attractive secretary.

systems ['sistəmz]: (science of) the organization required to make many different parts work together in an efficient whole.

tackle ['takl]: deal with, e.g. *tackle a job* = decide how to do the job and then do it.

tact [takt]: skill shown in dealing with other people without offending them.

tariff ['tarif]: a tax on imports.

tempo [ˈtempou]: rate, speed, e.g. the *tempo of change* = the rate at which things are changing.

time [taim]: – *from time to time* = sometimes.

trade union [ˌtreid ˈjuːnjən]: – see *union*.

transit [ˈtransit]: being carried from one place to another; goods *in transit* are on their way from seller to buyer; *transit goods* on their way to another country may be handled at a port like Hong Kong (Chapter 17).

turnaround [ˈtəːnəraund]: (time) between a ship's arrival in a port and its leaving with a new cargo, stores etc.

unanimous [juˈnanıməs]: with everybody agreeing.

unforeseeable [ˈʌnfɔːˈsiːəbl]: such as cannot be expected and cannot therefore be planned for in advance.

Union [ˈjuːnjən]: organization of workers for the defence of their rights. Each trade has its *Union*, or *Trade Union*, which is a member of the *Trades Union Congress* (T.U.C.).

urgent [ˈəːdʒnt]: requiring immediate action; a *matter of urgency* [ˈəːdʒnsi] is something that must be dealt with very soon.

utility [juːˈtiliti]: usefulness.

vacuum-pack [ˈvakjuəmˌpak]: a way of preserving food etc by removing air from the container in which it is packed.

venue [ˈvenjuː]: a meeting-place.

versatile [ˈvəːsətail]: able to do many different things; n. *versatility* [ˌvəːsəˈtiliti].

warehouse [ˈweəhaus]: a building for storing goods; *warehousing* [ˈweəhauziŋ] = storing goods, finding space for goods in warehouses.

wharf [woːf]: (plural: *wharves* [woːvz]) wooden or stone structure to which a ship can be tied to load or unload cargo.

works [wəːks]: factory buildings or the parts of them in which machinery is used; the *Works Manager* [ˈwəːks ˈmanidʒə] = the manager in charge of the manufacturing work of a factory.